3D Philanthropy

Make your donors love you by connecting with their minds, hearts and souls

Fraser Green

civil sector press

3D Philanthropy

IMPORTANT:

The following materials are intended as general reference tools for understanding the underlying principles of fundraising and relationships. The opinions expressed herein are solely those of the authors. To ensure the currency of the information presented, readers are strongly encouraged to solicit the assistance of appropriate professionals.

Further, any examples or sample forms presented are intended only as illustrations. The authors, publishers and their agents assume no responsibility for errors or omissions or for damages arising from the use of published information or opinions.

ISBN-10: 1-895589-89-4
ISBN-13: 978-1-895589-89-4

3D Philanthropy

Published by Civil Sector Press
Box 86, Station C,
Toronto, Ontario, M6J 3M7 Canada
Telephone: 416-345-9403
Fax: 416-345-8010

Publisher: Leanne Hitchcock
Editor: Lisa MacDonald
Design: Alan Tang

This book is lovingly dedicated to my soul mates:
Jacqueline, Rory, Jack and Jennifer.

In the lottery of life, I've been blessed with
incredible love from the mother, daughter,
best friend and wife I've been given.
You all planted many seeds
that brought this work to life.

Thank you.

Table of Contents

"Truth is relative to the time in which one lives and to the individual who can grasp it."
– *Gustave Courbet*

Foreword

If you want to really understand your donors, you must understand the simple truths of human nature. If you understand why people do what they do, you'll understand why your donors give the way they do. There's true elegance in that.

3D Philanthropy is the Mona Lisa of donor portraits. For the first time ever, donors are presented as the simple – and yet complicated - human beings they truly are. They think. They feel. They're capable of inspired giving and soulful generosity.

I preach the importance of donor loyalty and commitment to anyone who will listen. In today's philanthropic economy, there is no single engine that drives revenue growth more than truly loyal and connected donors. Fraser gets this. This book is really a donor commitment manual – full of practical tips and recipes to deepen donor connections and foster the loyalty that results. For that, we should all be grateful.

Fraser's genius is his understanding of what makes people tick. He shares his gift with us in this concise, penetrating and game-changing book. With his own unique brand of wit and charm, Fraser weaves simple stories together that lay before us the flesh, bone and blood of philanthropy. No mystery. No rocket science. Just a genuine and thoughtful enquiry into the all-important 'why' questions behind donor motivations.

This book will soon become required reading for novice and veteran fundraisers – not to mention CEOs and board members. It's time for all of us who work in philanthropy to give our donors the respect and care they deserve. That respect starts with getting inside the donor's skin and seeing the world through the donor's eyes.

What can you expect from *3D Philanthropy*? You can expect to laugh and chuckle many times. You'll probably cry at least once. You'll have nerve endings poked. Once you're finished, you won't forget what you've just read. This book will just hang around inside you – like the memory of your first true love.

This is a beautifully written book by someone who is passionate about people connecting with each other more deeply.
3D Philanthropy is a wonderfully human gift to each and every one of us who reads it.

Roger Craver
Martha's Vineyard, Massachusetts

Seven Philanthropic Truths

1. *Of all the animal species on earth, we humans are the most social. We exist and thrive in large part because of our relationships with each other.*

2. *The need in human beings to meaningfully connect with others is as primary to us as our needs for warmth, food, water and safety.*

3. *People relate to each other in three ways – intellectually, emotionally and spiritually. These three relational dimensions are present in all healthy people – and our behaviour reflects these dimensions each and every day.*

4. *Philanthropy is a natural extension of our healthy desire for others to survive and thrive.*

5. *People connect to each other philanthropically in their intellectual, emotional and spiritual dimensions.*

6. *Charities who connect fully (in all three dimensions) with their constituents have the highest probability of earning their loyalty and trust.*

7. *Loyal donors are the economic engine of philanthropy. They contribute the greatest proportion of net revenue to their chosen charities.*

Fraser Green, 2011

Chapter 1
The Three Dimensions
Wilf's Day in Three Vignettes

Donor Dossier

Name:	Wilf
Age:	62
Marital Status:	divorced
Profession:	high school music teacher
Children:	two adult daughters, one adult son
Religion:	Roman Catholic
Passions:	classical music (especially Baroque), reading, foreign films

Wilf goes to work

At 6:45 a.m. – just like every weekday through the school year – Wilf gets into the driver's seat of his Toyota, puts his coffee into the cup holder and turns on the ignition. And so his commute begins.

A few minutes into his drive, Wilf hears the traffic report on the radio. There's been an accident on the expressway and traffic is backed up as police and ambulance try to get to the scene.

"Damn!" shouts the little voice inside him. *"Why today of all days?"* Wilf has a rehearsal with his school band at 7:30 this morning. They're prepping for the spring city-wide music competition a week from Friday. He's going to be late and he knows it. As he reaches for his coffee he realizes that his hand is trembling a little. He takes a sip and tries to calm down.

After a moment, Wilf begins to collect himself. He takes another sip and says to himself, *"I'd better come up with plan B."* He decides to take the Richardson Side Road over to Highway 7. The route is slower than the expressway on a normal day – but with the accident today, it looks like his best bet. He picks up his Blackberry and calls the school office to leave a message that he expects to be twenty minutes late, and that somcone should ask the kids in the band to start their warm-ups without him.

Wilf lets out a big exhale and begins to accept that this morning's delay isn't the end of the world. He'll make the best of it and try not to let it rattle him anymore.

He turns on his CD player and begins to listen to the music. It's Mozart's Requiem – perhaps his favourite piece of music. His mother had chosen a portion of this piece to be played at her memorial service two years ago. At first, Wilf thinks back to that service and it brings back the sadness of her death and her last months, slowly deteriorating from the cancer. Her last day, lying in that hospice bed. Even after two years, Wilf often feels lonely – and kind of lost without her.

Then, he realizes that his phone is still in his left hand. He turns down the volume and calls his voice mail. He listens again to the voicemail message his daughter had left for him last night.

Ever since his divorce and his mom's death, his daughter Louise had stepped up and assumed a sort of mothering role with him. Calling him almost every day. Checking in to see if he's alright.

Louise called last night to invite him to dinner on Friday – and he'd saved the message. As he listened again, he marvelled at how Louise's laugh is a carbon copy of his mom's. He smiled, thinking of the similarities between the two – and how incredibly close they'd been. Despite the age difference, they'd always been kindred spirits. Sharing inside jokes with each other. Exchanging knowing glances at family dinners – which always looked to Wilf as though the two of them were speaking without speaking.

Wilf rolled down his window and could smell the river as he crossed the bridge. The sun had been up for an hour and the morning was warming up. He let his shoulders drop a little and kept thinking about Louise and his mom. About how he worshipped them both. How blessed he was to have them in his life. How he was the link in the generational chain that connected them. How the chain went back tens of thousands of years. And how it would continue – link after link, generation after generation – long after he's gone. He imagined grandchildren, and realized for the first time, how much he was looking forward to being a granddad.

His attention drifted back to Mozart – and allowed himself to be surrounded by the music. When he began thinking again, what a genius that man was. What a gift he'd given the world. What a legacy he'd left behind – a legacy that had lasted more than two centuries. In that moment, Wilf felt deep gratitude. For his mom and daughter. For Mozart. For this beautiful morning. Even for this detour along a country road.

Before he knew it, Wilf was pulling into his parking spot at Central Junior High. He looked at his watch – and realized he was only 8 minutes late after all. He grabbed his briefcase from the passenger seat and hurried into school.

There were 28 kids waiting inside - waiting to learn from him.

Wilf gets home

At 6:15 that evening, Wilf opened the back door of his house and stepped into the kitchen. He dropped his keys and briefcase onto the counter and called, *"Hamish!"* Instantly he heard the rapid clicks of paws bounding down the stairs. In an instant, Wilf's Scottish terrier was at his feet, furiously wagging his tail (or what tail he had). Wilf bent down to scratch Hamish's head, but Hamish threw himself up, rolled over in mid-air, and landed on his back on the hard ceramic floor. After a long day at home alone, a scratch behind the ears wasn't enough for Hamish – he deserved a full belly rub and he was going to have it.

Wilf laughed uproariously (as he always does when his dog does mid-air acrobatics). He gave Hamish his rub and headed to the cupboard to get out the kibble. As he filled up Hamish's food and water bowls, Wilf mentally reviewed his checklist for the evening:

- check the slow cooker to see how the chicken and rice is doing

- call Louise and confirm dinner on Friday

- review his lesson plans for tomorrow

- eat – but remember to take a smaller portion (Wilf's trying to lose twenty pounds)

- take Hamish for his walk

- watch the documentary on the life of Antonio Vivaldi on public television at 9 p.m.

- get to bed by 10 – there's another band rehearsal tomorrow and he needs to leave 15 minutes early to make sure he's on time.

A couple of hours later, Wilf and Hamish are strolling briskly across the football field at Riverbend Park. Wilf always looks forward to his evening walks with Hamish. A chance to let his mind wander. To begin to let go of all that happened during the day. To relax and wind down a little.

As they reach the trees along the river bank, Hamish picks up a scent and begins to tug on the leash. Wilf gives a quick correction tug and Hamish settles back into their pace.

As they walk along the path beside the river, Wilf looks across and is transfixed by tonight's sunset. The western sky has begun to turn from pale blue to shades of purple, red and orange. The sun is a deep golden ball, partly hidden behind the horizon. The wispy clouds have changed their shade from cottony white to slate grey.

Wilf pulls Hamish to a reluctant stop. Wilf gazes at the horizon. Transfixed. Peaceful. Without thought or worry. His body relaxes and loosens. He smiles – just a bit – without realizing it.

Five minutes later, the sun is all but gone. *"Come on Hamish!"* Wilf encourages. *"Let's get home and have a treat!"* At the sound of the word 'treat,' Hamish breaks into a trot and makes a beeline for home.

Wilf's philanthropic moments

The next evening, Wilf is sitting at his kitchen table. He's just finished his supper (leftover chicken of course) and is sorting through the day's mail.

He opens a letter from a breast cancer charity he's been giving to regularly since his mom got sick. The letter is from a man named Tom who lost his wife to breast cancer in 2006. Tom talked about his 28-year marriage, his kids, his love for his wife – and how much he still misses her. As he reads through to the end, Wilf feels a deep sadness. He knows how Tom feels. Both Wilf's mom and Tom's wife died too young. Both Wilf and Tom were grieving too soon. Wilf thought about the cancer charity. The annual report talked about encouraging research and new treatments. He'd looked at the financial statements and the organization seemed to be very well managed. Wilf decided not to send a cheque this time. He was going to make a monthly $25 gift from now on.

Just as he was filling out the form, his phone rang. When he answered, a young man launched into what sounded like a sales pitch for a charity that Wilf had never heard of called "Find the Missing Children".

Wilf tried to speak a couple of times, but the caller just kept going, sounding like he was reading a script. Finally, Wilf said *"I appreciate the call, but I've never heard of you folks. I give to several charities already, so I'll decline tonight thanks."*

The caller then kept speaking about six missing children in Wilf's city and said that if they didn't raise more money tonight, they probably wouldn't find them.

That was enough. Wilf interrupted with a loud and firm "*NO THANKS*" and slammed down the phone. "*What nerve!*" he thought to himself. "*Do they think I'm an idiot?*"

Wilf took a deep breath to calm down and went back to his mail. His next letter was from "The Blue-Green Project", an organization dedicated to ocean conservancy. This letter was from the Executive Director and it talked about some of the campaigns that they were currently waging to preserve ocean ecosystems and the species that lived in them.

The letter made specific reference to the killer whale and its migratory pattern up and down the west coast of North America.

Wilf suddenly remembered his mom's bucket list. When her cancer was diagnosed as terminal, Wilf's mother had made up a list of ten things she wanted to do before she 'kicked the bucket,' as she called it.

The biggest item on her list was to go whale watching off the west coast of Vancouver Island. She asked Wilf to take her the September before she died. That trip had been the last time Wilf had spent some real one-on-one time with his mom.

Wilf walked over to his desk and booted up his computer. He went to his personal folder and clicked on two of the videos he'd taken on that trip. His favourite was a one-minute clip of his mom practically hanging off the side of the boat to get closer to a mother grey whale and her calf – which were a stone's throw away. At one point she turned back to the camera, smiled this huge smile and said "*Isn't it beautiful Wilf? Isn't it beautiful?*"

Wilf wiped a tear from his eye and clicked on the bucket list he'd created the week after his mom's memorial service. Number four on his list of ten was "Go whale watching off Vancouver Island – in a kayak."

He closed his eyes for a moment and imagined the experience. One man in a small craft, all alone in a big ocean. Mountains in the background and a big cloudy sky overhead. Feeling how incredibly small we really are on this earth and in this universe. Wilf stayed 'in his kayak' for a few moments before he opened his eyes again.

He gave his head a little shake as if to wake himself up – and went back to the kitchen to get his wallet. He came back to the computer, found The Blue-Green Project's website, pulled out his VISA card and made an online donation.

Wilf in 3D

Let's go back through our three stories about Wilf and take a look at his dimensions. By that I mean the three planes in which he functions throughout his day.

Intellectual state: *When Wilf is having certain moments, he's in his brain. He's thinking rationally – and for the most part, clearly. Wilf's having his thinking moments when he:*

- hears about the accident on the freeway and comes up with another route he can take to work

- calls the school to tell them he'll be late

- makes his evening checklist at the dinner table

- thinks about the breast cancer charity's annual report and financial statements

- decides to give a monthly donation to the breast cancer charity and when he decides to make an online donation to Project Blue-Green

Emotional state: *When Wilf is in other moments, he's primarily in his heart. He's feeling emotions. Feeling and thinking are different. Let's look at Wilf's emotions in the brief stories you've just read. Wilf's heart is in charge when he:*

- first hears the news on the radio about the expressway accident and exclaims "Damn!"

- first starts listening to Mozart's requiem and starts thinking about his mom's passing

- laughs at Hamish's acrobatics and insistence on a full belly rub instead of a scratch on the head

- reads the breast cancer letter from Tom and thinks of his mom

- gets angry with the telemarketer who won't hear 'no' for an answer

Spiritual state: *These are the moments when Wilf transcends thoughts and feelings. In these moments, he's connected – either to a deeper self or to the broader universe. These are the moments of his pure essence – the heart of his onion with all the other layers peeled away. Let's review Wilf's stories and identify when his soul was in the driver's seat. Wilf is connected with his spirit when he:*

- listened to his daughter's laugh on voicemail and realized there is so much of his mom in her

- rolled down his car window, felt the sun and smelled the river

- got lost in the beauty of Mozart's music

- enjoyed his "sunset moment" while walking Hamish

- looked at the video of his mom and the whales

- imagined seeing those whales from a kayak.

So now, you've met Wilf and you've been introduced to the idea of the three dimensions of human existence. Don't worry if you don't fully know Wilf yet or if you don't feel entirely comfortable with the three dimensions of human experience.

The rest of this book will help you with all of it.

What you can do right now is look back over your day today – and perhaps your day yesterday. Go through them moment by moment, experience by experience – as best you can. Try to figure out which dimensions you were in under certain circumstances and in certain thought processes or behaviours.

But do it gently. Nothing in this book is intended to be so rigorous that it hurts!

Chapter 2

HEAD – The First Dimension

Donor Dossier

Name:	Bridget
Age:	53
Marital Status:	married twenty-nine years to Bruce, a philosophy professor
Profession:	director of nursing at Sunny Rest Nursing Home
Children:	three daughters – all in their twenties
Religion:	Jewish (non-practising)
Passions:	gardening (especially roses), chess, historical fiction, classic rock

Starting in the head

To begin our 3D exploration, we'll start with the easiest dimension – the head. By the head, I mean the brain – or more specifically that part of the brain also known as "the big brain", "the new brain" or – more neurologically, the neocortex.

This is the brain that gives humans our superior intelligence and reasoning ability. It is the seat of what neurologists call "executive function." Put most simply, this is the part of us that THINKS.

Bridget's day

5:30 A.M.

Bridget takes the tea bag out of her cup and sits down at the kitchen table. She boots up her laptop and puts on her ear phones. And so begins her daily half hour of online Spanish instruction.

Bridget's middle daughter Sinead is working with an international development NGO in Guatemala – and Bridget is planning a three week trip to visit her in March. She has decided that she wants to have a basic level of competency in Spanish when she's there – so every day she works on her tutorials. She finds it frustrating at times – but loves the thought of speaking a second language.

Bridget loves the sun – and is looking forward to many trips to the Caribbean and Latin America where her Spanish will come in handy.

7:15 A.M.

Bridget passes by the nursing station at Shady Rest Nursing Home on her way to her office. The desk nurse sees her coming down the hall and begins to chatter excitedly. *"Am I glad to see you! Mary-Anne's called in sick. Jennifer's going to be an hour late. Mrs. MacMillan is a half hour past her medication time and Mrs. Chaikovsky is refusing to eat her breakfast again."*

Bridget gets her to calm down – and spends the next five minutes prioritizing the outstanding jobs. The necessary assignments are made and everything settles down.

9:45 A.M.

Bridget looks up from her desk as Kirsten comes through the door. Kirsten is the CEO's admin assistant. *"I've got the draft budget for next fiscal Bridget,"* Kirsten says a little sheepishly. *"I don't think you're going to like it. Just remember not to shoot the messenger okay?"*

Bridget scans the budget and quickly zeroes in on her bottom line. Next year's budget has cut the nursing allocation by 14% - even though the expectation is that the amount of nursing care provided will be a little more next year. Bridget's been to this movie before – so she keeps her cool. But, she knows the nurses' union won't take any more cuts lying down. She's going to have a struggle on her hands in the weeks to come.

12:20 P.M.

Bridget packs up her lunch bag, reaches for her tea and picks up her copy of the Sunday *New York Times*. She flips to the chess column and reads about the scenario that's outlined.

She looks at the chessboard diagram, closes her eyes and imagines herself playing the black pieces.

She plans her next move – and then the next – and then (depending on how her opponent reacts) the move with her Queen that could turn the game decidedly in her favour. Bridget loves the complexity of chess. The combination of highly structured precision with the inherent unpredictability that a human opponent provides.

She glances at her watch, takes a last gulp of her tea and heads back to her office.

5:40 P.M.

Bridget turns off her computer and reaches for her coat. As she reaches for the car keys in her pocket, she begins her daily ritual of planning an efficient trip home. Pick up the dry cleaning. Stop at the market for baby spinach and lemons. Call her daughter from the car. Get to the gym in time for her step aerobics class. Drop her books at the library. Listen to the Bruce Springsteen mix that Bruce had downloaded for her on the weekend. And, if there's time, stop in on her mom (who lives just six blocks from Bridget's house).

Multi-tasking has been a part of Bridget's life for as long as she can remember. It's second nature to her – and she's good at it.

The incredible thinking machine

Our brains are miraculous pieces of machinery. Our senses absorb 11 million bits of information each and every second. You and I have some 60,000 thoughts every day. We are exposed to about 10,000 marketing messages on a daily basis.

We drive our cars without thinking. We engage in one conversation while listening to one or two others at the same time. We use a vocabulary of about 20,000 words – and there are another half million available to us (in English at least).

Our brains set us humans apart from our animal kin.

Somewhere about 100,000 years ago, modern humans emerged from Africa and began their migration to the Middle East, Europe and Asia – and later to Australia and the Americas. Our earliest ancestors can be traced to the Rift Valley in and around Kenya – including Lucy, a 3-million-year-old humanoid fossil.

As we evolved from Lucy's time to the time of the global migration, something pretty amazing happened. Our brains grew like crazy. They didn't just get bigger – they developed many specialized compartments capable of different intellectual tasks. Our intellectual capability is what sets humans apart from the 62,000 other species of vertebrates that share this earth with us.

Now, 3 million years ago, our ancestor Lucy (anthropologically known as an australopithecine) had a brain. But, her brain was much smaller and simpler than yours and mine. Her brain was primarily instinctual – designed to help her decide fight or flight from prey and predators. The ancient brain (also called the reptile brain, old brain, snake brain) was geared for moment-to-moment survival. Lucy's brain didn't read or write. It didn't have vocabulary. It didn't multi-task or play chess.

I think of the neocortex as the computer in my head. It's all about information. Inputs. Outputs. Exchanging information with others in my tribe.

Psychologists and neurologists refer to the big brain's job as "executive function." I like that description. My brain is up there in my head – wearing a charcoal grey suit and tie, carrying a briefcase, wearing glasses and looking very serious.

The list of executive functions is huge. Among other things, our brains:

- process language

- have mathematical capability

- can reason logically

- synthesize, synergize and combine different ideas and pieces of information

- plan for the future

- overrule instincts (like sex and violence) to maintain social cohesion

- correct errors

- create

- choose among multiple alternatives (an important one for fundraisers!)

- anticipate rewards and consequences

Unlike other members of the animal world, our big brains allow us to maintain large memory banks of past events (and their consequences) and to envision future scenarios that will depend on current behaviour. In fact, if you stop and think about it, you probably spend more of your day with your head in the past and future than you do with your mind focused on the present.

Big brains and the social animal

Our big brains have evolved the way they have for a very good reason. Like all evolution in all species, our brains are directly linked to our most fundamental drives to survive and procreate.

The big brain, in short, has turned humans into the most social of animals. Our genius as a species isn't in what any one of us can do. It's what we achieve as a group that has put us at the top of the animal hierarchy.

Our brains allowed us to create language. Language allowed us to share information, to plan, to settle differences without violence (sometimes) and to explore our world more fully.

Language has allowed us to teach, learn and study. We've formed the ability to specialize our individual skills and talents for the benefit of the tribe. As fundraisers, we're highly specialized in the economics of philanthropy. Even within our own field, some of us specialize in direct response, others in data management and others still in major and planned giving.

Despite our wars and criminal behaviours – our violence and vitriol – we are a remarkably communicative and cooperative species. Without our big brains, we'd still be grunting in cold, damp caves and eating our meat raw.

I would also argue that our social history is a major reason that philanthropy plays such a large role in today's economy and society. In Canada, where I live, the nonprofit sector accounts for about 10% of Gross Domestic Product (GDP) and a tenth of all employment.

I believe that our tribal programming extends to our innate understanding that we owe each other a certain minimum standard of existence. We also know rationally, that we risk what we have if we allow others in our tribe to live in fear for their very existence. For some, philanthropy is merely enlightened self-preservation.

Bridget the thinking donor

Let's go back and spend some more time with Bridget – and share some of her philanthropic behaviours that are driven by her big brain.

MONDAY 6:15 P.M.

Bridget drives by the Good Shepherd Centre on her way home from work. On the roof of the centre is a large billboard advertising "Christmas Dinner for only $2.97." She thinks for a minute, *"It costs me WAY more than three bucks to feed each person at my Christmas dinner table. That's a great deal."*

Bridget remembers that she received an appeal from the Good Shepherd in the mail last week. She decides to send a cheque tonight to provide 15 meals to the homeless this Christmas.

TUESDAY 10:30 A.M.

Bridget opens an email from her daughter's best friend. Michelle is preparing to go to work in Africa for two years as a volunteer with an international development NGO. Michelle is running an online campaign to raise $5,500 to offset her travel and training costs. She asks Bridget to make a contribution – and emphasizes that Bridget's donation will be matched on a 2:1 basis by the Federal Government.

Bridget decides to contribute $334 – and with the match, kick in $1,000 towards Michelle's campaign. She thinks that's great value.

THURSDAY 8:05 P.M.

Bridget sits on her sofa to open her mail. There's a big package from her community hospital foundation that contains a special donor report. The report lays out a two-page spread on where donor dollars have achieved results in the hospital over the past year. There are descriptions of pieces of equipment, scholarships for nurses and an expanded emergency department among other things.

Bridget is impressed by how much the foundation has achieved and as a nurse, understands how much patient care will benefit because of these improvements that donor dollars have made possible. Bridget makes a mental note to give a bigger donation to the hospital next year.

THURSDAY 8:25 P.M.

Bridget goes online to check out a new organization in her area that provides services to families who are caring for parents with Alzheimer's and other forms of dementia. She quickly navigates her way around the site. She's impressed with the Board of Directors – it's a smart combination of people with professional expertise and people from the business community who are well connected fundraisers. The medical advisory board has members that Bridget has known and respected for years. The Executive Director is a former colleague at the hospital Bridget worked at before she took the job at Shady Rest.

Bridget thinks the new organization's program and services are well thought out and very much in demand. She likes their goals. And, most of all, she knows that this organization recruited great leadership. She's learned from experience that organizations without strong leadership don't get far.

She clicks on the contact button to offer a donation and to volunteer her services.

Head stuff

I wrote my CFRE exam in 1997. In the months leading up to my exam, I joined a weekly study group here in Ottawa. We met at the Red Cross boardroom on Wednesday mornings and reviewed the books that were "going to be on the exam."

All the books we studied – and the exam that followed – were focused on the fundraiser's head and the donor's head. This is how fundraising was – and still is – taught. Facts and figures. Stats. Concepts and conventional wisdoms. All head stuff.

Now don't get me wrong. Head stuff is great. And it's definitely important. But it's only one of the three dimensions. Today, some fourteen years later, I think my education and certification were incomplete.

But I'm getting ahead of myself. I'll save my thoughts for the next two chapters.

Chapter 3

HEART – The Second Dimension

Donor Dossier

Name:	Caroline
Age:	36
Marital Status:	married nine years to Cal, a mortgage broker
Profession:	sales manager for a software company
Children:	two: daughter Anna aged 8 and son Max aged 5
Religion:	none (gets her spiritual information largely from Oprah Winfrey)
Passions:	long-distance running, cycling, ballroom dancing

While the brain is the seat of our reason and intellect, the heart is where our emotions reside. This is where we begin to separate what we think and what we feel. Let's meet Caroline and visit a day in her life to begin our emotional investigation.

Caroline's Day

5:40 A.M.

Caroline pushes the start button on her espresso machine and reaches for the newspaper on the kitchen counter. She sighs with the peace and satisfaction that she has about thirty minutes to start her day – before the craziness begins again.

Picking up her newspaper, Caroline notices a slip of paper on the counter. She picks it up. It's a note from her five-year-old daughter Anna, printed awkwardly in big red capital letters. The note reads "I LOVE THAT YOUR THE MOM I GOT. XOXO."

Caroline sighs again and smiles. Life may be nuts most days, but she wouldn't trade her kids for all the tea in China. She's blessed and she knows it. The espresso machine beeps – and Caroline snaps back into her day.

9:15 A.M.

Caroline is at her desk, ploughing through her email inbox. She looks up to see her boss leaning against the door frame.

"Hi Dan. What's up?" she asks.

Dan replies, *"Caroline, the first quarter numbers are in. Your sales were 18% over target – and your team had the top gross in the country - again."*

Caroline beams.

Dan continues, *"I've checked with head office. I want you to give your whole team the day off this Friday. And as for you young lady, I want you to book a week off next month. Consider it time in lieu for all the extra hours you put in to make this happen."*

Dan turns and strides away. Caroline sits there a little stunned – but very happy. She loves her job. She knows she's very, very good at it. And now she's got an extra week off. Sweet.

12:15 P.M.

Caroline puts her yogurt container and spoon down on her desk and has another sip of green tea. She picks up the phone receiver and calls her sister Joyce.

"Hey Joyce – how'd it go at the doctor's this morning?" Caroline asks.

Joyce's voice is uncharacteristically flat. *"The doctor is booking me for a MRI. She says there's a chance it might be cancer."*

Caroline gulps a breath. She puts on the brave face she learned from her father. *"I'm sure there's nothing to worry about J. Doctors always want to eliminate the most remote possibilities. Do you want to meet up at Starbucks after work for coffee? Cal's picking up the kids tonight so I've got a little time."*

They set their coffee date and Caroline hangs up the phone. She stares at the spoon beside the yogurt. She can feel her heart pound. The office suddenly feels warm.

For the first time in her life, she's afraid that her little sister might not live much longer.

5:15 P.M.

Caroline starts her car and calls voicemail on her cell phone. She listens to the message that's been left. It's from her dad.

"Hi sweetie. Just calling to see how you're doing and what's new. We missed you at dinner on Sunday. Hope you're well – and that your mom and I will see you and the kids soon. We miss you."

Caroline starts to drive toward Starbucks. She feels crummy. Her parents would do anything for her – and yet, it seems so hard to find any time to give to them. And, at this stage of their lives, all they want from her is her time – and time with their grandkids.

She feels guilty, and decides that they'll go to her parents' house for dinner this Sunday – come hell or high water.

6:10 P.M.

Caroline rushes through the front door and kicks off her shoes. She drops her brief case on the floor and runs upstairs to get into her running gear. She's got an hour before Max's homework time. Her husband Cal is picking the kids up from daycare and doing dinner tonight – so Caroline has a precious hour for herself.

In the bedroom, she notices that the message light is blinking on the phone. She calls voicemail and the message is from Cal. *"Honey, I'm REALLY sorry, but I forgot that this was my night to pick up the kids. It's 6 o'clock on the nose and I'm just leaving work now. Can you go get them and get supper started? I'll be home as soon as I can, depending on traffic."*

"DAMNIT" she thinks to herself. *"Does he think I can do this all by myself? What an ass! I'm SO sick of this."*

Caroline runs back down the stairs to put on her shoes and grab her keys. She knows the kids are going to be grumpy about being the last to be picked up – again.

9:45 P.M.

Caroline is on her home computer – doing a quick Facebook check-in before bedtime. She hears a soft 'mew' from behind. She turns to see Sniggles limping toward her.

Sniggles is the family's cat. He's fourteen years old, almost blind and very lame from arthritis. Caroline rescued him from the SPCA when he was a kitten. Caroline had just graduated from university and was starting her career in sales.

Sniggles had been her roommate in that tiny studio apartment downtown. Her companion and confidante. The kids both love him like crazy – even though he spends most of his time in his little bed under the dining room table these days.

Caroline picks him up and strokes his neck. The vet says that Sniggles' arthritis has become very painful. He recommended that they think about putting him down.

But Caroline's not ready to do that. Not just yet. She blows softly into his ear and feels very sad. She's going to miss him so much.

Our emotional wiring

As you read Caroline's mini-stories, you probably related to some (if not all) of them.

These moments in Caroline's day reflect the various emotions we experience pretty much each and every day.

What are emotions? Where do they come from? And most importantly perhaps, why do we have them?

Last Christmas, my wife Jennifer gave me a very cool gift. It was a DNA-based testing service that traces my genealogy back through tens of thousands of years. So (just like CSI Miami) I swabbed the inside of my mouth and sent the little kit off to be tested.

I received my results a few weeks later. My ancestors trace back to Egypt some 50,000 years ago. By 25,000 years ago they had migrated around the Mediterranean to the Balkan Peninsula (probably today's Serbia, Bosnia and Croatia). Later still, they migrated to Scandinavia – and probably on to Britain or Ireland. (How cool is it to be descended from Vikings!)

But to get to the root of emotions, I have to go back at least to my Egyptian roots – and probably even further back than that.

Our emotions aren't really based in our hearts – although we use the heart symbolically to represent their physical home. Our emotions come from a small, walnut-sized mini-brain at the top of our spine called the amygdale (pronounced ah-MIG-da-la). The amygdale is also known as our 'ancient brain', our 'reptile brain' and our 'snake brain'.

As we saw in the last chapter, the 'big' brain that occupies most of our skull space is called the neocortex. Evolutionary speaking, the big brain is a much more recent innovation in human history. It's a very different organ – with very different functions.

But, let's get back to that snake brain of ours...

Every living species on earth – from dandelions to earthworms to humans – has two primary drives. The drive to survive – and the drive to reproduce.

Our emotions are our ancient survival and procreation programming if you like. Those programs were developed – through Darwinian trial and error – over thousands of years. Our ancestors experienced successful emotional evolution – and we are the proof of that by our being here.

Now, I'm not a neuropsychologist. But I'm going to give you my layman's understanding of our primitive programs – why we have them – and how they operate today.

The emotional solar system

I've been a self-taught student of human emotions for about eight years. I've read dozens of books and spent countless hours on the internet trying to understand what makes us tick – to understand why we do the (sometimes ridiculous) things we do. Here's my take.

Our emotions have evolved to help us do two things:

- to seek out those things (like food, warmth and sex) which help us satisfy our survival and reproduction drives, and

- to avoid those things that threaten our survival or ability to reproduce.

Let me present the emotional array this way. Imagine a solar system:

- The sun at the centre of the solar system is your emotional self (the heart).

- There are four major planets that orbit the heart – each with a number of moons. They're like Saturn and Jupiter. They're big and powerful.

- There are also two smaller planets further out in the heart-sun's orbit (like Neptune and Uranus) – but they don't have moons.

There are many interpretations of our emotional solar system. There is wide agreement among the experts on the four big planets that follow. To mix metaphors, you could think of them as the primary colours of the emotional palette.

1. *Happiness:*

In our drive to survive and procreate, we have learned over many millennia to be attracted to those things that improve our well being. We have learned to feel good feelings associated with those things that actually increase our odds of making it to the next day. Things like

- just finishing a great meal.

- being warm and safe and cozy.

- being acknowledged or appreciated by our group (which could be friends, kin or tribe).

- lying back after amazing sex.

- feeling the warm sun on your face.

We all want to be happy. Happy is the "best" of the four primary feelings. It's where we want to get to – and once we're there, it's where we want to stay. Most of us go to great lengths to 'get to happy'.

Sometimes we go to ridiculous lengths to find happiness. I'm sure that – like me – you've planned a vacation. You've, booked your precious week off work, travelled a long way, spent a lot of money and maybe put up with some jet lag – only to find that you don't feel so wonderful at the end of the rainbow. Your travel mates are bitchy. You're tired. The coffee sucks. You get lost. You get the picture. The point is that we want to be happy and that we'll go to great lengths to find the feeling.

Or, imagine this. Fifty thousand years ago, my Egyptian ancestors were sitting around the fire in the evening after their meal. Someone tells a funny story and everyone laughs uproariously. That laughter causes everyone to let go of all the day's tension – to recharge their human batteries and prepare for the sleep to come. In that moment, my ancestor is safe from crocodiles and warring tribes in the neighbourhood. She can just breathe and take it easy.

Remember that I described happiness as an emotional planet with moons? The many moons of the happiness planet include contentment, satisfaction, excitement (the good kind), enthusiasm and optimism to name a few.

2. *Sadness:*

This emotion is associated with loss. When we lose something – or someone – important to us, the emotional result is usually sadness. We feel sadness because we believe that which we've lost is important to our survival and/or ability to procreate.

The saddest experience of my life was when my mom died. Even though I was a mature 44 year-old man with a child of my own, my mom's passing made me feel very lost, lonely and vulnerable. An indescribable emptiness. The feeling that an important part of me was no longer there.

My Croatian ancestors 25,000 years ago probably felt sad losing babies in childbirth, losing sons and brothers in battle and coming home with nothing to show for a day's hunting. The evolutionary source of this feeling was that losing the baby or failing to kill some prey put one's survival at greater risk.

The moons around sadness include loneliness, depression, melancholy and emotional "tiredness." These are all offshoots of the same fundamental feeling of having lost.

3.   *Anger:*

Getting really peeved is also an emotional tool that was very helpful in our ancestors' drive to survive and procreate.

Anger is about incursion onto our space. About something being taken from us that is rightfully ours. Or, about the threat of something being taken from us.

I know that my most common 'anger trigger' is when I feel that I'm being taken for granted. When I don't feel appreciated or valued. When I believe that someone else doesn't recognize my efforts or my very presence.

Anger often comes from a judgement that an injustice has been done – and that the person who did the injustice deserves some sort of retribution. Anger is often driven by a desire to 'even things out'.

One of my Viking ancestors may well have felt anger plundering an Irish seaside town. Perhaps he felt like someone else in the raiding party had taken a bigger share of the loot. Perhaps he spotted a woman he wanted to take for a wife – but another Viking wanted her too. They could well have had a major punch-up over her.

The moons of the anger planet include frustration, resentment, impatience and outright rage.

4. *Fear:*

This is perhaps the strongest of the four primary emotions. From the time knuckles were dragging on the ground, those of us who survived had learned to be very fearful of that which could cause us to perish. Those of us who were lazy with our fear were eaten by very large cats.

It stands to reason that – if our survival is the bottom line – that death is the biggest fear of all. Therefore, we're most afraid of those things that could end our lives. I think that's one reason why so much of what makes the news involves death. For people of my generation at least, the very word cancer evokes instant fear – because we equate the word cancer with the word death.

My ancient ancestors would have lived in a state of constant fear and vigilance. They had to avoid predators. Neighbouring tribes could be warlike. Added to that, they had no idea what kinds of catastrophes the gods had planned for them next. In ancient times, those phenomena which couldn't be explained were simply attributed to the gods. That's why so many civilizations, from the Romans to the Mayans, went to great lengths to appease their gods. They were taking out insurance policies against floods, fires, pestilence, earthquakes and outbreaks of mysterious diseases.

In fact, some people of faith still describe themselves as 'God-fearing' to this day.

For as long as I can remember, my greatest fear has been failure. That fear has driven me to be a high achiever and a people pleaser. My recurring dream (that I've had hundreds of times since I was a young child) involves trying to do something simple – like get to my hockey game – but being confronted with an impossible string of roadblocks and obstacles. This fear of failure has played a huge role in shaping the person I am today.

I've thought about my fear of failure a lot. Why do I have it? What am I really afraid of? After many years of pondering, here's my best Dr. Phil take: I'm afraid that if I fail at something, my 'tribe' will disapprove of me. If they disapprove of me, they might cease to care about me and abandon me. If I'm left abandoned, I won't be able to survive on my own – and I'll die. That may sound ridiculous, but I honestly believe that my fear of failure follows that primitive emotional logic.

The moons around the fear planet are many – and include anxiety, nervousness, shyness and embarrassment.

The moonless planets

There are also two 'non-primary' emotions that orbit your heart's sun. When I was first learning 'emotional intelligence' these were not considered primary emotions. As I read further, I found that some psychologist-types use only the previous four – while some others include the two that follow.

Because of their relevance to philanthropy and giving, I'm going to include them – but you can be the judge as to whether they belong.

Gratitude:

We feel grateful when we have received something important. It may be a physical gift – or it may be simple appreciation for our behaviour or for our very being.

My Egyptian ancestor would have experienced great gratitude at the successful birth of a child or the sight of her husband with a nice, fat antelope slung over his shoulders.

Gratitude, in evolutionary terms, is important I think because it keeps us focused on what really matters to our survival and procreation. It is also usually an exchange between people – whether family members or fellow tribesmen. We show gratitude to "keep it coming". We receive gratitude and want to 'keep bringing it'. Win-win baby.

In most spiritual and religious traditions, gratitude is a part of our practice. Giving thanks is a part of our social and religious culture.

Two years ago, I became a step-dad to an amazing five-year-old boy named Thomas. For our first year together, much of our "Thomas training" involved reminders to say thank you. As parents, we feel it's so important that our children thank others promptly, consistently and appropriately.

I happen to be a yoga guy. I take many classes in many places from many teachers. At the end of each and every class, I make it a point to wait until the instructor is alone and thank her. Our boys are also expected to thank their coaches after every basketball practice. This simple act reminds us of what others do for us – and how others make our lives more worth living.

In North America, we even have a statutory holiday dedicated to the act of thanksgiving.

I have one more thought on thanks. We as humans simply LOVE to be thanked. When we are thanked, we are recognized. We're shown appreciation. We're made to feel like we're important – like we matter. We humans are a highly social species. Being recognized and appreciated by our fellows is important to us – and this is very deeply wired in our old brains.

Guilt:

This is another "negative" feeling that we experience for very good reason. Guilt helps us survive.

Feeling guilty is the result of a behaviour we've done that has harmed another. As social animals, we need each other for our mutual survival. We need to respect each other and care for their well being as well as our own. Guilt is, if you like, an automatic corrective emotion that helps us stay on the straight and narrow of peaceful coexistence.

Since pre-history, we have been programmed to have this feeling so that we'll get along in some sort of harmony with our fellow family and tribe members. The flip side of the guilt coin is often a desire to do something to 'make it right' to the injured party.

Just as Jennifer and I have taught Thomas to say thank you to show appreciation, we're teaching him to apologize when he's been selfish, thoughtless or inconsiderate. We're teaching him to be a connected member of his family and tribe.

In the Jewish tradition, Yom Kippur is one of the highest of holy days –observed by practicing and secular Jews alike. Yom Kippur is the Day of Atonement. It involves prayer, fasting and other observances geared to "making it right" with God.

With atonement comes forgiveness – and forgiveness is a central tenet of many religions and cultures. We're working with Thomas to be as quick to forgive as to say he's sorry when he's done wrong.

When we're forgiven, the weight of guilt is lifted. We're given a new chance. A fresh opportunity to survive and procreate.

Back to Caroline's day

Let's take a minute now to go back to the start of this chapter and review some of the emotional moments in Caroline's day.

- At 5:40 a.m. Caroline discovered Anna's "I love you" note under her newspaper and felt a surge of <u>gratitude</u> for her wonderful kids.

- At 9:15 a.m. she feels incredible <u>happiness</u> when her boss praises her work and gives her and her team the reward of some time off.

- At lunchtime, Caroline is struck with <u>fear</u> when her sister tells her she's going for diagnostic tests to check for cancer.

- At the end of her workday, she feel <u>guilty</u> when she listens to her dad's voicemail message, and realizes that she's been neglecting her parents.

- When she gets home, Caroline feels a surge of <u>anger</u> at her husband for forgetting it was his day to pick up the kids at daycare and start supper.

- Before going to bed, she feels a twinge of <u>sadness</u> when she contemplates that Sniggles the cat is nearing the end of his earthly journey. She's going to miss him.

I've included Caroline's 'diary for a day' to illustrate that our emotions are with us many, many times each and every day. In the preceding section, we looked at why we have emotions in the first place – and why they were programmed so deeply into us.

The confounding thing about our emotional makeup is that the purposes for which we were programmed with them – survival and procreation – are rarely the reasons we experience them today. Yet, our emotions exert powerful sway over what we think and how we behave.

You and I are still pretty much the same people who paddled our rafts down the Nile River 50,000 years ago. Our lifestyles and circumstances have changed a great deal. We have knowledge and access to information that was unimaginable just a century ago. But – and it's a big but – our emotional wiring hasn't changed much. Those impulses still fire as strongly as they did many millennia ago.

And all that ancient emotional programming makes us complex, confusing and oh so interesting!

Emotional characteristics

So what are the components of emotions? What do they have in common? (And as we'll begin to see in the next chapter, how do they differ from spiritual characteristics?)

There are three fundamental ways in which I believe emotions share commonality:

1. *Emotions are temporary:* Have you been deliriously happy for all of the last month? Have you been sad non-stop since last Tuesday? Have you been living your life in fear since Christmas? My hope is that your answer is no.

The simple truth is that emotions come and go. An emotion may stay with you for seconds, or minutes – or sometimes even hours. But they are temporary by their very nature.

2. *Emotions are responsive:* Our emotions for the most part just come and go out of nowhere. They are in fact "lit up" by events, thoughts and interactions. Going back to Caroline's day; her note from Anna sparked her gratitude, the praise from her boss triggered her happiness, her sister's call sparked her fear – and so on. In other words, emotions happen because something happens.

   It's an interesting task to sit down at the end of the day and review it from start to finish. Which emotions did you feel? When? What triggered them? How long did each one last? If you do this little exercise, you might be surprised to realize just what an emotional animal you really are.

3. *Emotions can be manipulated:* Here's another exercise for you. Make a little list of the people (and perhaps pets like Sniggles) who know how to 'push your buttons'. Many of us in close relationships know the other so well that we are able to push buttons like pressing keys on a piano keyboard. We know how to make our kids fear us. How to irritate our spouses. How to make our parents feel guilty. You get the idea.

   When you were a kid, you learned how to (sometimes at least) manipulate the emotions of your parents, your siblings, your friends and your teachers. You found that if you could trigger the right emotional response, you'd get the outcome you desired. Your parents let you stay overnight at your friend's house. Your teacher let you off with a warning instead of a detention. Your big brother didn't beat you up. We learn this stuff when we're very young – and we hone our skills throughout our lifetimes.

Emotions and philanthropy

So let's turn this chapter briefly to philanthropy and fundraising.

I'll start by saying that, in my experience, the most emotionally intelligent fundraisers I come across tend to be direct marketing copywriters and really good major gift people. The copywriter is a master storyteller who can make the reader 'feel close and personal' even though she is one of thousands reading the very same thing. The major gift genius knows how to read eyes and body language – constantly reading non-verbal cues as to the prospect's emotional state. (The least emotional group of fund-raisers I know tend to be planned giving people who focus on taxes, giving vehicles and financial planning.)

It's not hard to see how emotions can be powerful motivators for giving. Let's run through some examples of how charities and causes can focus on emotions to generate a response:

- A child sponsorship organization focuses on the monthly reports that sponsors receive every month telling them how happy their 'children' are at their new schools.

- An environmental organization shows footage of ducks covered in gucky oil because a tanker grounded itself near an environmentally sensitive coastline. We watch and feel anger at the oil company's greed and stupidity.

- A hospital tells us about how overcrowded its emergency department is – and how long patients are waiting for emergency care. We learn this and feel frightened that this might happen to our kids.

- You read an ad in the paper from your local homeless shelter leading up to Thanksgiving weekend – and realize just how fortunate you are to have everything you need to live a happy life.

- You get an email talking about the plight of Sudanese refugees and feel guilty that you've known about this humanitarian crisis for months – and have done nothing about it.

- You read a piece of mail from a grandmother whose granddaughter suffers from cystic fibrosis. You identify with that grandmother and feel very sad for her.

In the chapters to come, we'll explore the tools we can use to bring emotions more to the fore. Hopefully, at this point, you've come to appreciate that our emotions are ancient and VERY deeply wired into us.

Our modern Western culture doesn't really value emotions the way it might. Certainly many males (and females too for that matter) are raised to put a lid on our emotions – for to show them is to show weakness. So, as very young children, we learn how not to cry, how not to shout for joy and how not to tell our friends when we're afraid.

We may have learned how to hide our emotions – but they're still there.

Trump card

When it comes to human behaviour, emotions trump intellect just about every time. The heart rules the head.

Surely you can think of many times when you've 'let your emotions get the better of you'.

Maybe you yelled at some poor clerk in the hardware store. Maybe you cried in front of your kids. Maybe you told your wife how worried you were about losing your job. In those moments, emotions rule.

I'll close by asking you to do one more thing. Stop for a moment and think about the two most important moments of your life. They might be the birth of a child, the death of a loved one, the moment you said 'I do' at your wedding or the time you swam with the dolphins. Now, relive that moment in your mind as vividly as you possibly can. And answer me this: In that moment, were you thinking? Or feeling? My bet's on feeling.

Chapter 4

SOUL – The Third Dimension

"RUN YOUR FINGERS THROUGH MY SOUL
FOR ONCE, JUST ONCE, FEEL EXACTLY WHAT I FEEL,
BELIEVE WHAT I BELIEVE, PERCEIVE AS I PERCEIVE.
AND FOR ONCE, JUST ONCE, UNDERSTAND."

– AUTHOR UNKNOWN

Donor Dossier

Name:	Sheila
Age:	74
Marital Status:	widowed three years ago, after a happy 48-year marriage
Children:	four daughters aged 36 to 51
Occupation:	retired teacher, part-time bridge instructor
Religion:	raised Methodist, doesn't attend church regularly
Passions:	bird-watching, reading, her grandchildren, volunteering

Of our three human dimensions, the soul is the one that lies deepest within us. The soul – or spirit – is the core of our human onion, buried beneath the many layers of thoughts and feelings. It is more powerful than the head or the heart – yet it is also the least understood.

Understanding the soul and how it works is an opportunity for us to know others (including our donors) much more deeply – and to connect with them much more powerfully.

A week in the life of Sheila

MONDAY, 10:15 A.M.

Sheila steps out of the front door of her condo building, smiles and gives a friendly wave to the cab driver that's waiting for her. She climbs easily into the back seat, says good morning and gives him the address she's going to. He pulls away from the curb – and Sheila's thoughts begin to drift.

Sheila is going to her daughter Sara's house to drop off a birthday gift for her youngest granddaughter, Megan. She is almost nine and Sheila can't wait to help her celebrate.

Sheila thinks of that precious little girl. Her bright brown eyes. Her easy smile – and the way she chuckles so often at the little things she finds interesting or amusing. The way she's always exploring things – and asking those incessant questions. In all her years of raising kids and teaching kids, Sheila has never known a child as curious as this one.

Sheila gazes out the cab window and for some reason starts to reflect on her grandmother. Granny was such a vibrant, lively woman. When Sheila was a girl, she so looked forward to her family Sunday's at Granny and Granddad's. Granny was smart and talkative and so much fun to be around. She seemed to be enthusiastic about everything – and always had time to teach Sheila how to make a pie, to read to her in their "special corner" in the parlour or to sit quietly and wait for the baby robins to poke their heads out of their nest.

It dawns on Sheila that Megan and Granny are actually two peas in a pod. The same brown eyes. Both almost elf-like in their body shape and movement. And, both with that little chuckle. Sheila recognizes that, in a way, Granny and Megan are the human bookends of her life – spanning five genera-tions. She feels deeply connected in that moment – to her past, her present and to a future she won't be here to see.

WEDNESDAY, 2:55 P.M.

Sheila walks through the front door of the Spring Court Hospice. She smiles and says hello to the receptionist and heads straight up the stairs to the second floor.

She enters a room and breaks into a bright smile. Sheila says hello to Julie – a 42 year-old woman who's bed-ridden with ALS (Lou Gehrig's disease). Julie is in her last weeks of life and Sheila has come to read to her.

Sheila has been a volunteer at Spring Court since she retired from teaching in 2003. She spends one afternoon a week at the hospice, spending one on one time with terminally ill patients.

Sheila reaches into her bag and pulls out a copy of *The Piano* by Michael Nyman. She finds the book mark and begins to read aloud to Julie. As Sheila reads, she interjects with her own commentary, as if she and Julie were having a book club conversation. She also pauses here and there to brush the hair from Julie's face or to re-arrange her pillow.

An hour or so later, Sheila puts the book down and leans in close to Julie. Sheila looks deeply into Julie's eyes and smiles. Sheila draws a very long, slow breath and remains still. She focuses her thought (if you can call it thought) on sending love and warmth from her heart to Julie's.

After a few moments, the corners of Julie's mouth turn up ever so slightly. She's "heard" Sheila's message.

Sheila packs up her stuff and heads down the hallway to the staff kitchen. She plugs in the kettle to make some tea and settles into the moment. She knows she's doing good work. She's doing what matters. She's giving to another human being without any expectation of something in return. In that moment she feels very complete – and very worthwhile.

THURSDAY, 10:42 A.M.

Sheila turns the corner and continues her walk along Corkery Avenue. At the corner she climbs the steps and enters St. Bartholomew's Church. She finds a pew down the left aisle and takes her seat. She draws a long, slow breath and centres herself.

Sheila has come this morning to say good-bye to an old friend.

The church is almost full. Everyone has come to pay their last respects to Jack McCullough. Jack was once the Principal at the school where Sheila taught. He was a warm and generous man who loved the kids and held his teaching staff in high regard. Jack had been a mentor and good friend to Sheila. She was sorry to hear of his passing.

The priest begins the funeral sacrament. As he speaks, Sheila's mind drifts to her own thoughts about life and mortality. She imagines her own memorial service – and thinks of what would be said about her – and what her life had meant to others.

Then, she closes her eyes and prays silently to her Creator. She expresses thanks for her life. Thanks for her joys and sorrows. Thanks for the abundant love – and all those who'd shared it with her. Thanks for her knowledge and experience. Thanks for her serenity and contentment.

She asks that she be given the opportunity to use whatever time she has left well – being kind and loving to herself and others. She wishes for peace, wisdom and love for everyone who shares this moment on earth with her.

When Sheila finishes her short prayer, she keeps her eyes closed a few moments longer. She feels peaceful and ready to accept whatever the next moment – and the rest of her life – may bring her way.

SATURDAY, 6:12 A.M.

Sheila reaches into her knapsack and takes out a blanket. She spreads the folded blanket on the ground, which is still damp from the dew. She reaches in again and pulls out her binoculars. She crosses her legs and sits quietly.

Sheila waits. Her breath is almost imperceptible. She is still and quiet. In her mind, she is becoming a part of the hillside. She waits patiently.

Soon she hears the familiar call of a male cardinal. She looks to her right and sees him fly into a cedar tree. Looking more closely, she sees his mate between the branches. They're building their nest in the same spot they did last year and the year before. She smiles. These cardinals have been her 'friends' for six years now. It's good to see them back again.

Sheila maintains her silence. Then she hears another call and slowly lifts her binoculars. She begins to slowly scan the trees on the other side of the stream. After five minutes or so, she detects movement and focuses her binoculars on the spot. And there he is! A male Baltimore oriole! She watches him closely as he flits from limb to limb in a sugar maple tree. She is the silent witness of this rare event – blended into that little stream valley on this beautiful May morning. In all her years of bird-watching, this is the first Baltimore oriole she's sighted in her own hometown. Sheila pulls her little notebook out of her knapsack to record the sighting.

An hour or so later, Sheila packs up and begins to walk back up the path to her car. She walks with soft steps so as not to make any more sound than necessary. She is in a state of connectedness with all around her. Her day has started incredibly well. She is completely alive and content - and as she walks, Sheila breathes and listens to the life that surrounds her.

Your human core

If I had to choose one word to associate with my soul, it would be 'connected'.

To me, my soul connects me in two directions:

- I feel deeply connected to my deepest, inside self – or –

- I feel strongly connected to the universe that surrounds me – as if I have become one with it.

I would add a couple of secondary words or ideas to provide some harmony to the melody of connectedness:

- Soulful moments are often <u>quiet</u> and still. Buddhists talk about quieting the monkey brain. I love that expression. In truth, your brain is in an almost nonstop conversation with itself. Consider the fact that you have something like 60,000 thoughts each and every day. When we get soulful, that chatter slows way down.

- In soulful moments we let go of thinking and feeling and (at the risk of sounding overly Zen-like) <u>we just be</u>. We don't try to manage or direct. We just let whatever's happening happen. Our awareness is heightened somehow.

I think of my soul as my human centre. My core. My essence. It's what makes me me. It's what connects me to myself – and to my world. My soul is the source of my joys, my peace and my love. It's the most important part of this man I see in the mirror every morning.

A different kettle of fish

When my daughter Rory was about 8 years old, I was driving her to school one morning. At one point her voice chirped out of the back seat *"I know what the difference between happiness and joy is daddy."*

"Oh boy," I thought to myself. *"Of all the kids in the world, I had to get the philosopher."*

I collected myself and said *"That's cool sweetie. What IS the difference?"*

"It's easy," she said. *"Happiness comes from the outside. Joy comes from the inside."*

To this day (some fourteen years later) I have no idea whatsoever how she came up with that. But it's one of the wisest and most profound things anyone has ever said to me.

At first, it's a little hard to delineate the domain of the soul from that of the heart. And in truth, there is no clear solid line between the two. Having said that, I believe there are defining characteristics that help us separate the heart from the halo:

- Our emotions are clearly rooted in our Darwinian search for survival and procreation. Elements of the soul are more metaphysical than that. The journey of the soul is the journey of being human. It is the path to our full human potential.

- Emotions are temporary. They change many times a day. We get up every morning having no idea how many times we'll get angry or feel happy. Our soul characteristics are much more long-term and consistent. They are at the core of our personalities, our characters and our human identities. You may be sad right now and deliriously happy in an hour. You won't change from being highly empathetic to cold and uncaring that quickly. Soul characteristics often last a lifetime.

- Emotions are almost always triggered by people or events. You get angry looking out the window to see the rotten weather. You're thrilled when your son tells you what a wonderful mom you are. Our soulful moments can also be triggered, but in a different way. A soulful moment usually happens when you allow the channel of your spirit to be fully open to experience the joy, the peace or the beauty of this moment's experience.

- There's also a difference to the physical experience between the two – at least the Zen disciple in me thinks so. Emotions at the physical level are often sharp, brief and intense. Soulful experiences are broader, deeper and last longer – kind of like an ocean wave that washes slowly over you and stays there awhile.

Past, present & future

There's another important differentiator between emotional and soulful experiences – and that difference is driven by tense.

Emotions are often focused on the past or the future. You're sad because you found out yesterday that a friend is very sick. You're happy because a colleague asked if you'd lost weight fifteen minutes ago. You're afraid of what the boss is going to say about you at the staff meeting tomorrow afternoon. The vast majority of our emotional moments are spent dwelling (sometimes needlessly) on what's happened in the past – or in what will or might happen in the future.

Spiritual experience happens right here – right now. Soulful experience happens in those all-too-rare moments when we let go of both the past and the future and simply lose ourselves in the present moment. Great soul moments happen second by second. Your sense of time seems lost in those moments because suddenly time seems so irrelevant. When you held your baby in your arms for the very first time, do you have any idea how long you held her before giving her back to the nurse? I'll bet the farm you don't. You were lost in a moment of deep connection. The length of time of that moment is immaterial. The depth of the human bond that was formed in that moment was everything.

God & soul – religion and spirituality

I'm feeling the need to insert a bit of a disclaimer at this point. This chapter is about your soul. Your human spirit. Your essential mojo .

This chapter isn't about God (with a capital G) or religion at all.

Religions are spiritual organizations that always include some form of hierarchy and some set of rules. Religions over time become institutions of one sort of another.

The third dimension of human connection doesn't go there. You don't need a priest or a rabbi to speak to the soul of another. You don't need a mullah or a swami to deeply connect with your true self.

Spirituality and religion to me at least are quite distinct. Religious people are often – but not necessarily – spiritual. Spiritual people can be – but certainly don't have to be – religious.

Having said all that, The Gallup Organization has been polling Americans for decades on religious beliefs. In the USA, 90% of the adult population believes in God, 80% believes in Heaven and 70% believes in Hell.

In Canada, a 2008 Harris-Decima poll found that almost three-quarters of Canadian adults believe in God. In the UK, 2001 census data shows that 70% of Britons believe in God. So, whatever you or I choose to believe – or not believe – the majority do believe in God.

Searching for soul

This spiritual stuff is pretty esoteric to many of us. So let's get as practical as we can about it. Where and when do we find our spiritual moments? When do we know when we're there?

Here's a brief list of some of the elements that can bring me into my spiritual dimension:

- *Places can be spiritual.* In the tradition of the Yaqui Indians of Mexico, warriors set out on a type of vision quest to find their own personal places of power. In the Yaqui tradition, a warrior goes to his power place to gather his energy and strength – and to compose himself in trying times.

  I have found special places in my life that seem to have the power to restore me. One such place is a foot bridge the crosses the Indian River in the Mill of Kintail Conservation Area – about ten minutes from my house. The small river runs quickly below that bridge – and the water runs freely even in the dead of winter. My mom's memorial service was held just steps away from that bridge. It was a special place for her too.

  This is a spot where I feel peaceful, quiet and able to just listen to the world. In the here. In the now.

- The old saying goes that "beauty is in the eye of the beholder" – and there's little doubt that's true. The Irish philosopher and writer John O'Donohue said that "beauty is the illumination of the soul." I fully agree with him. I, for example, am almost hypnotized by sunrises (much more so than sunsets for some reason). Watching the beauty of a sunrise seems to connect me deeply with the universe in which I exist.

- *Words have great spiritual power* – even though the soul is for the most part a non-verbal component of our deepest self. When I read or hear someone express profound thoughts and ideas, I feel my experience expand.

John O'Donohue (whom I've just mentioned) is a great example of such a wordsmith. O'Donohue was born in County Clare, Ireland, trained to be a priest, went on to become a Hegelian philosopher – and ultimately became known to the world as an interpreter and populariser of Celtic spirituality. He is probably best known for his authorship of Anam Cara – a Book of Celtic Wisdom.

For my money, John O'Donohue is the most beautiful writer in the English language. His words have magic in them. They shine a flashlight on the deepest parts of me.

- *Sounds can have a profound effect on my spirit.* I'm an auditory learner, and have always found that I have a deeper attraction to sound than many around me. Music is a form of spiritual expression to me. I love to sing. I have two guitars and a banjo. Sometimes I sit alone and play without intent. My fingers just wander off and make their own music. That is spiritual release and surrender to me.

  I find many sounds spiritual. The call of a robin early in the morning. The sound of moving water soothes me – as does the sound of the wind rustling leaves. Reading aloud to someone somehow creates a deeper bond between us.

- In my experience, *certain people can act as spiritual catalysts.* Have you ever met someone for the first time – and very quickly feel like you've known that person all your life? Have you ever re-connected with an old friend after many years – only to find that you picked up your friendship as if no time had passed since your last conversation? Have you ever been smitten by someone in just seconds?

  These people often turn out to be our soul mates and fellow travellers. If you've ever read *Anne of Green Gables*, you'll remember how Anne enthusiastically exclaims to Diana Barry that they are kindred spirits

– sharing a bond that others can't possibly know or fully understand. Anne gets the idea.

- In the Reiki tradition, we ground our souls to one or more of the four elements – water, air, fire and earth. By grounding, I mean centering and calming yourself – and pulling your fragmented thoughts, feelings and spirit closer together into the coherent whole which is you. I have found through practice that I ground most to air, and then water. Air grounders like me love mountain tops – and the seeming closeness to the sky. I ground least to earth – but my reiki master will go out into her back yard in the wintertime, take off her shoes and stand on the frozen ground in her bare feet to feel grounded. Now, standing on frozen ground in your bare feet in the middle of a Canadian winter seems kind of nuts to me – but I don't ground that way!

Let's try and make a practical example that might make sense to you. Imagine a really great afternoon at the beach. You're lying on your towel in the sand (earth). The sun (fire) is warm and bright on your face. The breeze (air) on your skin feels gentle. The rhythm of small waves (water) lapping at the shore nearby sounds like a lullaby. You relax deeply in that moment on the beach, even though you're not sleepy in the least. That's big-time grounding.

Your soul triggers are probably very different than mine. Maybe you connect with pottery – feeling your fingers moulding wet clay. Planting annuals into your garden. Seeing the first robin in springtime. Or looking at a Monet painting and losing yourself in the image for a moment.

Whether your soul triggers are puppies or kittens, babies or old folks or hearing Bach's Brandenburg Concertos – my point is that there are places, people, sights and sounds that trigger spiritual experiences in all of us.

Immortality

"The true meaning of life is to plant trees, under whose shade you do not plan to sit."
– Irish immigrant (to Canada) farmer Nelson Henderson

A major part of almost all spiritual traditions and religions involves the metaphysics of the soul beyond physical life. Almost all believers – from Muslim to Methodist - cling to such ideas as the eternal soul, heaven and hell and karma and reincarnation.

Developmental psychologist Erik Erikson (1902-1994) achieved fame by identifying nine stages of human psychological development. In Erikson's schema, we must successfully achieve each stage in order to graduate to the next. Those of us who successfully climb this ladder achieve (more or less) our human potential.

Late in life, the most well-developed of us achieve a stage called 'generativity' where we form the ability to love those who will never love us back. We do good works in order to build a good future in which we will not take part. Or, to plant a tree in whose shade we do not plan to sit. This – albeit in an indirect fashion – can be argued to be a form of immortality too.

What's love got to do with it?

So, where does love fit? Heart or soul?

I'm about to go up against cupid, Valentine's Day and about a thousand pop songs that would suggest that love – in our 3D context at least – is a heart/emotional matter.

I disagree. I firmly believe that love lives in the soul. To make my case, I'll bring a handful of expert witnesses to you – the love judge and jury:

- Aristotle said that "Love is composed of a single soul inhabiting two bodies."

- Folklorist and anthropologist Zora Neale Hurston said "Love makes your soul crawl out of its hiding place."

- Victor Hugo wrote, "Love is a portion of the soul itself."

- Deepak Chopra says that "Anyone who has fallen in love has had a spiritual experience."

- None other than Saint Augustine declared that "Love is the beauty of the soul."

- I'll call William Shakespeare as my last witness. He said "When love speaks, the voices of all the Gods make heaven drowsy with its harmony."

Love to me almost defies definition. Having said that, I'll do my level best to try to frame it.

Thinking back to the neurological wiring of our ancient ancestors, there's an obvious place for love in terms of survival and procreation. The procreation part goes without saying. When I think of the survival part, I think of a mother's love for her child, or a man's love for the mother of his children. We humans are highly tribal animals. We have always depended on others for our very survival. That's probably why in some societies, banishment from the tribe is the most severe form of punishment that can be meted out to someone who breaks its laws and norms.

- When I look at the people I love the most, I ask myself – would I pay any price to save that person if she was in mortal danger? If the answer is yes, I believe the love between us is very deep.

Let's go back to what's already been said about emotions and soul. That emotions are temporary and largely externally driven – while our soul characteristics are much more consistent and deeply ingrained. I have loved my daughter since the day she was born. I have not had days where I felt indifference to her. I will love her deeply till the day I die. My love is deep and durable. That kind of love doesn't belong with the heart. It lives and breathes in the deepest recesses of my spiritual dimension.

My personal belief is that love is the primary reason for our existence. That giving and receiving love is the most meaningful experience we can have in this life. For that reason alone, love resides in my soul.

History & anthropology

I know full well that many of you reading this chapter are feeling pretty itchy by now. Most of us don't spend a lot of time or energy thinking or talking about our spiritual selves. Some of you might think I'm some sort of new age nut-bar (and maybe I am!).

I would ask you to take a broader look at it though. Those of us who live in the affluent western part of the globe are somewhat of a recent, societal anomaly.

Spirituality and/or religion have been a dominant force in human society throughout all of human history. And, spirituality is still a dominant force in many societies around the globe today (India comes to mind as an obvious example.)

The greatest civilizations on earth have all revolved around gods, beliefs, ancestor worship, rituals and maintaining spiritual equilibrium in the world. The Greeks. The Persians. The Egyptians. The Mayans and Aztecs. The list goes on and on – across millennia and across continents.

The Romans for example employed spiritual professionals called augurs. Ancient Romans would never consider opening a session of the Senate or staging gladiatorial games of any kind without the augur consulting the gods and declaring that the auspices were favourable for such an event to begin. (If the auspices were poor, everyone was sent home.)

Those of us in post-industrial North America and Europe are caught at an extreme swing of the human history pendulum – where material security and gain is seen as the ultimate measure of life's success. In human historical terms, this emphasis on material well-being puts us in a very small (and some would say impoverished) minority.

God and philanthropy

The market research I've been involved with over the years has taught me many valuable truths about philanthropy. One of the important truths I've learned is that people of faith are far more philanthropic than their non-believing neighbours. In our direct mail donor profiling for example, we've found that Canadian direct mail donors are three times more likely to give if they attend religious services with some regularity compared with the general adult population.

In the summer of 2010, I read a fascinating book by Deepak Chopra titled *How to Know God*. His fundamental thesis – as I understand it at least – is that there are seven broad ways that people and societies relate to the Creator. To me, they follow like rungs on a ladder.

The first rung is the God of survival. In ancient societies, people would pray to their God(s) for rain or sun or an end to pestilence. They were asking God to allow them to survive. The second rung is the God of rules. This, to me, is the classic Old Testament God who passed the Ten Commandments to Moses. The patriarchal God who lays down the law for His children.

The seventh – or highest – rung is the God of One. At this stage, we come to know that we are one with each other and that we are all one with our Creator.

I love this stage seven God. There's such a natural link between this interpretation of our Higher Power and philanthropy. If we are all one – if we are all God – we give. I give to the poor child in Burma because she is God. I give to the homeless guy standing at the off-ramp because he is God.

Beautiful stuff.

Soul brother, soul sisters

I remember coming across a quote once that said something like "Love is the mutual recognition between souls." I love that. While there are many people that I love in my life, there are five that I believe I am connected deeply with at the level of my soul.

- My mom and I were (and I suppose in a way, still are) soul mates. We had this unspoken connection. We knew when we were thinking the same thing at the same time. In some ways, we were incredibly alike. There was always an unspoken knowing between us. The sense that trying to hide something from the other was wasted effort. I adored my mom – and I'm pretty sure it was mutual.

- I also feel a deep connection to my sister Barb. She has one of the most empathetic, generous and caring souls of anyone I know. Most people who know her go on about how brilliant she is – and she's a genius indeed. But when I see Barb, I don't see her intellect. I see the incredible love she radiates. The warm energy she transmits to me and to those in our presence. That's why, when I was married on New Years in 2010, Barb was my "best man".

- When I started grade ten, there was a new kid at school. Jack McCullough had just emigrated with his family from Belfast, Northern Ireland. For some reason, I decided to put my wing over him and help him get acclimatized to Renfrew Collegiate. We've been best friends ever since. Jack and I share many passions, including music, sports, laughing till we hurt, pondering life and being in nature. Jack lives on Vancouver Island – and we see each other rarely. But when we do, it all comes back in an instant. Come to think of it, Jack is the one person who knows my journey from adolescence to the man I am today better than anyone – even though we may sometimes go a year or two without exchanging a word.

- Even though she hates it when I say it, my daughter Rory is indeed my life's masterpiece. In my years on this planet, I've done nothing more meaningful and rewarding than being her dad. The baby I held in my arms in 1988 is now a confident, capable and compassionate woman. She loves herself, makes great decisions and has pretty clear sense of her path. She is (alarmingly) mature, poised and has a wonderful way with people. She is indeed my mom's legacy in so many ways.

A couple of years ago, I was on a business trip to Vancouver. I stayed the weekend so that Rory and I could spend some time together. On Saturday morning, we decided to drive up to Whistler for the day. In no time, Rory fell asleep in the seat beside me – and she slept for most of the 1 ½ hour trip.

At one point, I looked over at her. I saw her face – and I saw my baby's face – at the same time. I turned and looked back at the road in front

of me. But I fell into a few moments of deep happiness and contentment. Just having her beside me was such a source of joy for me. As
I write these words, that feeling comes back. Powerful, peaceful and
beautiful all at once.

- On a freezing, dark night in November 2007, I was sitting in a dim
sum restaurant on Somerset Street in Ottawa. I was on my first date
with a woman named Jennifer Benedict, and as we talked I found
myself becoming more and more intrigued. This was a woman I found
REALLY interesting. She was funny and confident. She was obviously
very bright. She had gorgeous green eyes and an amazing smile (which
she revealed sparingly at first.) She also had a pronounced spiritual
side which included yoga, reiki and meditation practices.

I started to think that I'd just hit the dating bull's eye.

After dinner, I decided to take a risk. I drove to a place called Remic's
Rapids. It's a stretch of the Ottawa River, not far from Parliament. At
this particular spot, the water is only inches deep, and it runs quickly
over very flat layers of limestone. Out in the shallow water were
dozens of stone sculptures that kind of resemble inukshuks. Jennifer
and I walked in the biting wind to the shore. I pointed to the shadows
of the sculptures out in the water. We stood there in silence for a few
minutes. Then, feeling more than a little embarrassed, I suggested we
walk back to the car.

As I turned the key she said "Those were amazing. I can see why
they're so special to you. Thank you for showing them to me."

I was hooked. She got it. She got me. A little over three years later,
Jennifer is my wife, my best friend, my lover, my confidante and my
soul mate. She knows me better than anyone on earth. She knows
layers of me that no one else will ever know. That kind of knowing
doesn't happen in the brain – or in the heart. That kind of knowing
happens when two souls connect – truly, madly, deeply.

Philanthropic soul

So how does the soul connect with philanthropy? Good question.

Let's start with the word philanthropy itself. From the ancient Greek, it means "love of humankind". As we've already established, love resides in the soul. It stands to reason then that acts that demonstrate our love of humanity are acts from the soul.

Every human civilization and culture that I'm aware of has within it a tradition of helping others in need – or charity for the less fortunate. I remember once seeing a poster on the wall in a hospital hallway. This poster showed the vast array of religious traditions (from Christian to Epicurean to Hindu to Zoroastrian) and quoted their holy scriptures on the subject of coming to the aid of our brothers and sisters in need. Now, I was raised in the Christian tradition, and one of my first lessons was the 'golden rule', do unto others as you would have them do unto you. That poster had about twenty versions from as many faiths – but they all basically said the same thing.

When it comes to motivators to give, the three dimensions can all be triggers. We can make the intellectual decision to buy 10 Thanksgiving dinners at the homeless shelter because it only costs $30 – and that's great value. We can watch an infomercial from an animal welfare society and feel so sad at the sight of the poor abandoned kittens that we call the 800 number with our VISA card in hand. But there's no question in my mind that our most meaningful giving – both in terms of its human and monetary value – comes from the soul.

Sheila's soul giving

Let's close this discussion by returning to Sheila, who we met as this chapter began:

Tuesday, 2:45 P.M.

Sheila is sitting with her financial planner, reviewing her investment portfolio. Her net worth has just surpassed $1.5 million – largely because of the current value of the home she bought with her husband in 1964 and the summer cottage they built when the girls were young. She tells her advisor that she wants to commemorate her husband's memory by endowing a chair in civil engineering at the University of Edinburgh, where he'd been educated. She also decides to leave 10% of her estate to the local Conservation Authority – a nonprofit organization that protects the watershed of the river where she loves to go bird watching.

Thursday, 10:15

Sheila sits at her kitchen table, sipping tea and reading the latest report from a child sponsorship agency she's been supporting for more than 30 years. Included in the mail package is a letter from Indira, her latest sponsored child in Mumbai, India. She smiles at the photo of Indira, thinking back to the hundreds of children she had taught in her own classrooms during her career.

Sheila picks up the phone and calls the agency. She wants to arrange a gift whereby Indira and her brothers and sisters will have their sponsorships guaranteed until they all finish their education.

Saturday, 10:50 P.M.

Sheila and her daughter Stacey stand and join in the standing ovation taking place in the auditorium. They have been in the audience to enjoy a performance of Swan Lake staged by a visiting ballet company from Chicago. She remembers her first ballet – her granny had taken her to see the Nutcracker at Christmas in 1944. Sheila fell in love with ballet that day – and her passion for it stayed with her throughout her life.

On the drive home, she decides to call the ballet company on Monday to see how she could best support their capital campaign to restore the auditorium.

During this particular week, Sheila has made four very soulful gift decisions. She's honoured her soul mate and partner of 48 years by endowing a university chair in his name. She's expressed her passion for bird watching by supporting the organization that protects their habitat (hopefully so that her granddaughter will find the same passion). She made the child sponsorship guarantee because of the love she'd exchanged with so many wonderful students during her teaching days. And, she decided to support the ballet company in the hope that future generations would have the opportunity to appreciate the beauty of dance.

Late one night, Sheila puts down her novel and reaches to turn off the bedside lamp. It's been a long but very fulfilling day. Sheila lies back in the dark and closes her eyes.

Then, without really thinking about it, Sheila begins to quietly recite:

> "Now I lay me down to sleep,
> I pray the Lord my soul to keep.
> If I should die before I wake,
> the Lord my soul to take."

She smiles to herself and thinks "*Where in the world did that come from? I haven't said that prayer since I was a little girl.*"

Sheila rolls over, plumps her pillow and drifts off.

65

Chapter 5

The people have spoken!

Okay.

I've just spent four chapters (and about 15,000 words) rambling on and on about the three human dimensions of head, heart and soul. Obviously they're important to me (writing a book is a LOT of work after all). But, that's not what really matters.

Are these three dimensions important to the people that matter - your donors?

You bet your boots they are.

Do your donors even know that they have these three dimensions? Yep, they do. And I've got some data to prove it to you.

In the fall of 2010, my partners at Good Works and I conducted an online panel of 700 Canadian donors. We asked a variety of questions that were a little out of the ordinary.

Most surveys ask about giving – with questions like:

- How do you give?
- How much do you give?
- How often do you give?
- Who do you give to?

You get the idea.

We wanted to take a deeper look at Canadian donors – so we asked some questions that - to our knowledge – had never been asked before. We knew we were rolling the dice – and that our answers might turn out to be totally inconclusive.

But, we hit the jackpot. And, truth be told, it was the results of this research project in late 2010 that convinced me to write this book.

We asked a few of "think" questions and found that:

- A slight majority of donors THINK that Canadian charities have become "too professional" in their fundraising practices.

- Three-quarters of the 700 donors surveyed THINK that charities should be run in a very businesslike manner.

- One third of the donors surveyed told us they have more than just money to offer to the charities they support.

I want to go on a bit of a tangent here and talk about trust.

A big part of our wiring for survival is the need to feel safe. I've already talked about how we humans are highly social animals – and how our survival depends on others in our tribes.

Trusting relationships are a huge part of feeling safe. And I would argue that donors want to feel a high degree of trust in the charities they give to and relate with.

Our online panel found some fascinating information on the trust issue that I want to share with you.

- On the one hand, 90% of donors surveyed felt that the charities they support do an effective and efficient job of getting their money to those in need. This suggests that your donors feel a pretty high level of trust in you.

- On the other hand, almost seven donors in ten (68%) say that the charities they give to could do a better job of telling them where the money goes and the impact that their donations have.

Sounds to me like they trust you – but not THAT much! Those charities that set about to build greater trust through better reporting and stewardship will garner more trust, loyalty and ultimately, money.

- Let's get back to questions that delve into the emotive and spiritual dimensions of giving.

We asked some questions that went beyond THINK – and into the domains of the heart and the soul. Here are a few compelling examples of what we found:

- Almost everyone we surveyed (95%) told us that it FEELS good to give to charity. Feeling comes from the heart – not the head.

- There was an overwhelming majority (84%) who said that their charitable giving is an extension of their HEART and SOUL. (How explicit can you get?)

- Four of five donors surveyed (78%) say that their charitable giving is an extension of their SPIRITUAL beliefs.

- Finally, we asked respondents to agree or disagree with the following statement: *"I believe in my heart that helping another human in need is an ESSENTIAL PART of my being human."* Guess what? More than nine of ten donors (93%) were in agreement.

"I rest my case. Humans are three dimensional. Donors are three dimensional. Not only do your donors live – and give – in 3D, they're well aware that they do."

My goal with this book is to persuade you to want to reach your donors more deeply by connecting with them in all three dimensions. The chapters that follow are about HOW to do it.

Come along for the ride. I promise it'll be fun.

Chapter 6

Connecting with the 3D's

Passionomics & The Holy Grail

So maybe it's time we have a talk about money.

You are a fundraiser after all – and this book's purpose is to help you improve professionally.

So, let's turn our attention to money – and why connecting with your donors' three dimensions is going to impact your bottom line.

Money makes the world go round

My academic training – at least the first part of it – was in economics. A big part of the economist's craft is calculating the relative scope of things, and then figuring out how changing different factors affects the bigger picture. It's kind of like high school science experiments with money.

For example, what does lowering the prime interest rate mean to the mortgage rates offered by banks? What do lower mortgage rates mean to new home purchases? How do those new home purchases affect construction industry employment? And how does increased employment affect the amount of income tax collected by the federal government?

I'm sure you get the idea.

I tend to look at the business of philanthropy this way – at least sometimes. How many of your first-time donors make a second gift? How many of your active donors from last year will make a gift again this year? How many gifts will the average donor make this year? How big – on average – will those gifts be?

At the end of the day, any quantitative analysis of your fund-raising program has to focus on two fundamental elements:

- the investment you make in your donors – namely, what you spend, and

- the revenue you get from those donors over time.

This is classic business-type return on investment (or ROI) analysis. Coca-Cola measures its ROI. So does Apple. So does Disney. So should you.

How much would you bid for this busload of donors?

I come from a direct response background – and direct response marketing is very much based on data, statistics and ratios. Being able to manipulate seemingly small numbers can have a dramatic effect on the success or failure of a campaign.

Let's take the example of a charity that does a direct mail donor acquisition (or prospect) campaign. They mail 100,000 pieces and hope for a 1% response rate. At the end of the day they want to measure how many first-time donors they brought onto the file – and how much they had to invest to bring those donors in the door.

Without going into all of the detail of it, here's a key nugget. If that charity can lower its cost per package by a DIME, it saves $10,000 on its campaign cost – and the cost of each new donor brought in is reduced by $10. These kinds of metrics can make the difference between success and failure in a campaign such as this.

The most important metric used in the direct marketing world is lifetime value. This is simply a measure of how much a donor is "worth to you" over his or her lifetime.

Let's look at a scenario I use sometimes in seminars:

> I have a busload of 50 donors outside in the parking lot. Each one of these donors is going to make 1.3 gifts of $45 per year for the next 7 years. I'm now going to auction these donors off – what should you bid?

> I can turn the question over to you – but make it easier. Each donor I just described is going to give a total of $409.50 in his 'lifetime' with your organization. The busload is worth $20,475.

How much would your charity pay for those donors? I'll leave that one with you to ponder.

Lifetime value

Let me turn the busload question around a bit – and give you a new scenario. This one involves identical triplet sisters who are all donors to your charity:

- Janice makes her gifts to you through the mail. She stays active with your charity for four years before she lapses. Her average annual gift is $40. Janice's (gross) lifetime value is $160. This is pretty typical.

- Joanne starts out the same as Janice and gives the same amount through the mail – except that after four years she converts to monthly giving. She stays on as a $14 per month donor for another 8 ½ years before she eventually lapses. Joanne's lifetime value is $1,588 – ten times the value of her sister!

- Jacqueline starts out the same as her sisters with four years of direct mail giving. She then follows Joanne with 8 ½ years of monthly giving. But, Jacqueline does something more. She decides to leave 5% of her estate to the charity in her will. When she dies, Jacqueline's estate is worth $400,000 – so her bequest is $20,000. Jacqueline's total lifetime value to your charity is $21,588.

Jacqueline's value is 13 times greater than Joanne's – and 135 times greater than Janice's!

Fundraising's holy grail

Over the past decade, there's been a trend that's been very disturbing to fundraisers pretty much across the board. It's getting harder and harder to renew donors from year to year. In my work, my partners and I have seen our clients strive (and sometimes struggle) to maintain (let alone grow) their donor renewal rates.

Make no mistake. Your donor renewal rate is probably the most important metric in your overall return on investment formula. Having a great renewal rate means that your program can run very efficiently – and you'll probably have a sweet bottom line at the end of your fiscal year.

On the other hand, a low donor renewal rate is a migraine headache for any fundraiser. You need to keep bringing in more and more new donors in order to replace attrition. This problem is compounded by the fact that attracting new donors is more difficult – and expensive! – than it's ever been.

In my opinion, a lot of charities today are casting around for new ways to "make it like it was before." Many are turning from the mail and phone to online fundraising and social media with very unrealistic expectations. Others make big investments in face-to-face fundraising only to find that a huge percentage of new donors quickly change their minds and cancel their monthly giving. Then, there's always the ever-popular strategy of adding another special event or two into the program mix in the hope of generating some quick cash – and then wishing that these event donors will become annual giving regulars (which they rarely do).

One of my favourite people in the philanthropic universe is a guy named Roger Craver. Roger began his fundraising career when I was in grade school – and he's still at it. He was a pioneer in direct mail in the 1960s, early into telefundraising in the 1970s, one of the first to get serious about online giving – and as I write this, he is pioneering charitable giving using mobile communications devices.

I first came across Roger when I was a political organizer in the 1980s. The trade magazine of the political campaign manager crowd was a magazine called *Campaigns and Elections* that was published in Washington. Roger used to be a regular contributor to that magazine with great articles about political fundraising. I quickly became a fan.

Over the last decade, Roger and I have become colleagues, peers and fellow travellers. I consider him to be a friend. He is a mentor to me – and one of the few people I call when I'm wrestling with something really big and important in my mind. His advice is always valuable – and his perspective on things almost always amazes me.

Three or four years ago, Roger and I started up a conversation on donor loyalty. He was becoming increasingly convinced that donor loyalty was a critical issue to fundraisers – and that the issue of loyalty was little understood in our sector. Roger and I have drafted loyalty surveys for donors, shared thought papers with each other and generally synergized on ideas, thoughts and potential solutions.

It was Roger who first coined the phrase, "Loyalty is the Holy Grail of Fundraising."

I've never agreed with anything related to fundraising as much as I agree with Roger's statement.

If you're a fundraiser and you're not obsessing with the question of improving donor loyalty, I honestly have to ask you where your priorities are. No question, no issue, no goal could be more important to us in today's philanthropic economy than loyalty.

British fundraising academic and brainiac Adrian Sargeant laid it out perfectly in his book, *Building Donor Loyalty.* In it, he states that a 10% improvement in a charity's renewal rate can lead to a 50% increase in net revenue. Think of it. If all you do next year is reduce your donor attrition by ten percent, you can add fifty percent to your bottom line. Now, that's focus!

(psst – it's not just donors!)

The dissolving of loyalty isn't unique to philanthropy by a long shot. Loyalty is eroding everywhere.

Customers aren't loyal to brands like they used to be. I remember when I was a kid, my dad would stand out in the driveway and chat with neighbours. Often, his male friends would say things about their cars like "I'm a Chrysler man." Those men in the 1960s defined their identities in part by the cars they drove. They wore their brand loyalty like badges on their chests. That kind of loyalty is pretty much a thing of the past.

Today, we switch brands like we change our underwear. When I think of my own life, I realize that I shop at different grocery stores, buy my afternoon Americanos at different coffee houses, rent movies at different outlets and buy books, clothes and music from different sellers.

There are very few brands to which I would say I'm fiercely loyal. Why should I be? I'm always scanning the marketplace for the vendor who can give me the best product at the best price with the most convenience. Simple as that.

As I was writing this chapter, there was a federal election campaign underway in Canada.

A generation ago, the VAST majority of voters simply stuck with the same party. Typically, a citizen made his or her party choice in early adulthood – and then voted the party line throughout his or her life. Back in my first career as a political campaign organizer, I was acutely aware that only about 20% of the electorate would 'swing' from one party to another – and that targeting swing voters was the key to winning. Today, that 'swing slice' is way bigger than I could have imagined just twenty years ago.

Here's a personal tidbit from this election campaign. I have been a lifelong NDP voter and activist. I'm a social democrat through and through – and my social democratic values are an integral part of my very soul.

During this campaign, the CBC ran an online poll called "Vote Compass." You would go online, answer a bunch of questions about issues - and the compass would tell you which of Canada's five political parties you're most closely aligned with.

So, I went to the CBC site and took the five-minute survey. Imagine my surprise when I was told I was a natural Green Party supporter!

I live in a constituency where the NDP doesn't really have a chance of winning. In my area, it's always a contest between the Liberal and Conservative Parties. In the past, that didn't make any difference. I would have voted NDP regardless of how poorly I expected my local candidate to finish.

In this election, I must admit that my primary 'election issue' is my desire to replace our current Conservative Prime Minister. I don't like him. I don't like what he stands for. And I don't like how be presents Canada to the world. He embarrasses me. He frustrates me. He angers me.

In this campaign, I'm actually having thoughts about voting Liberal. At the end of the day, I'll probably still vote for 'my' party. But, for the first time, in my life I've questioned my political loyalties. Hmmm...

The loyalty industry

The corporate sector has tuned into the loyalty issue in a big way. Customer loyalty has turned into a multi-billion dollar industry worldwide. I've just checked on Amazon.com and a search for titles on "customer loyalty" has turned up more than 1,000 titles!

Isn't it odd that when I substitute "donor loyalty" for "customer loyalty" in my Amazon search, I get 13 titles – and three of them are different versions of the same book!

"We in philanthropy haven't yet tuned into the loyalty issue – and we need to."

And from an economics perspective, that's what this book is about.

Loyal donors renew and upgrade. Your loyal donors are that 20% (or less) of your file who give you 80% (or more!) of your revenue. Finding ways to build and keep loyalty with your donors is probably the most important use of your mental bandwidth for the foreseeable future.

Market fragmentation and loyalty

Let's turn our attention to the two primary reasons for the erosion of customer and donor loyalty.

The first is the incredible fragmentation of markets that has happened in my lifetime.

Remember the little story I told earlier about my dad's neighbour saying he was "a Chrysler man?" Well, that conversation happened in the mid-1960s – when there were basically three auto manufacturers (Ford, General Motors and Chrysler) to choose from.

Less than a decade later, the OPEC oil embargo shot gasoline prices through the roof. Suddenly the North American auto market was flooded with little, efficient cars made by Toyota, Nissan (they were called Datsuns back then) and Honda.

Today, if I were to make a thorough list of the new vehicle choices available to me I honestly don't know how long it would be. My choices today include Mitsubishi, Kia, Saturn, BMW, Volkswagen, Lexus, Volvo, Saab, Land Rover – and on and on and on.

I grew up with three TV stations. My daughter grew up with hundreds. My parents had two newspapers to choose from. I have dozens – not to mention online news media like the Huffington Post.

There are more than 80,000 registered charities in Canada today. Off the top of my head, I can think of about twenty cancer charities alone – and I'm sure there are many more than that.

In short, market fragmentation has made it easy not to be loyal. If you're at all disappointed with your car or your newspaper or your last pair of jeans you can just switch brands. There's no guilt or angst. You just go out and find a better deal.

Generational cohorts and loyalty

The second big reason for loyalty erosion is the demographics of age.

When I started my first job as a professional fundraiser in 1989, the philanthropic market was dominated by the World War 2 generation. This is the age cohort that was born before 1946. Back then, the youngest member of this cohort was 43 years old. The WW2 generation dominated charitable giving – and if you could connect with this generation, you'd be just fine.

Demographers tell us that one of the defining characteristics of this generation is – you guessed it – loyalty. These are the donors who feel an obligation to give to "their" charities year after year.

They give from a feeling of duty – and if they don't give this year, they feel guilty about it.

That was then. This is now.

As I write this, the very youngest of that WW2 generation has turned 65. Three younger cohorts – Boomers, Gen Xers and Millennials are now swimming around in our philanthropic pond. Each generation is unique. Each has its own characteristics, values, motivations and behaviours.

But, the three newer generational cohorts have one thing in common: They simply don't display the same loyalty as their parents (or in the case of Millennials, their grandparents).

I want to be clear about this. I'm not saying that members of these cohorts can't be loyal. Of course they can. But their loyalty is much harder to earn – and once you have it, you cannot take it for granted. Not even for a minute.

The loyalty game has changed. The bar has been raised way up. We need to re-strategize and re-energize ourselves so that we can tackle loyalty in newer, more meaningful and thoughtful ways.

Framing loyalty expectations

Even if you focus every moment of your time on building loyalty, you'll never achieve a constituency made up entirely of loyal donors. Even if you possess loyalty genius, you won't get everyone to board your loyalty bus.

So what kind of goal should you set?

The answer of course is, it depends. It depends on what kind of cause you work with. It depends on how quickly you've grown over the past few years. It depends on the number of direct competitors you have to contend with in the marketplace.

But, as a general rule, I'd say that you should start out by setting the goal of achieving true loyalty with about one-quarter of your donor constituency.

This is my intuitive estimate – but it's a good place to start. As you think more about loyalty – and begin instituting loyalty strategies and tactics – your loyalty goals will become clear to you. But, for now, about a quarter of your donors is a great goal to start with.

The architecture of a loyal pyramid

A lot of my peers think that the fundraising pyramid metaphor is passé. I disagree – and I'd like to use the pyramid now for a minute.

Let's take a charity called Save the Pussycats Canada (STP).

STP has 10,000 annual donors who give via mail, phone and/or email. Their average donor gives $40, once a year. STP's annual gross income from their annual giving program is $400,000.

But STP wants to grow that pyramid using a loyalty strategy – and more importantly, a loyalty culture. They go out of their way to speak to their donors' minds, hearts and souls. STP fundraisers do everything possible to create deep connections with their donors – and to encourage donors to commit deeply to the cause and to the organization.

After five years of loyalty strategy and culture, here's what happens at STP Canada:

- 750 donors have converted to monthly giving at $15 per month
- 300 donors have stretched their giving to the $500 level and 100 have gone to $1,000 per year
- 250 donors have put STP into their wills at an average gift of $20,000.

Save the Pussycats Canada's revenue picture (annualized) now looks like this:

- the donors who haven't upgraded are still giving $338,000
- monthly giving income is $135,000
- those 'intermediate' ($500 to $1,000) donors give $250,000, and
- bequests (amortized over 20 years) represent $250,000 annually.

In this scenario, STP's annual income has gone from $400,000 to $973,000. STP has more than doubled its annual revenue without expanding its donor base.

This is how loyalty gets leveraged – and why loyalty matters to each and every one of us.

From transactions to connections

There's a big, hairy idea being revealed here.

It's audacious and elegant. It's freaking scary too.

The idea is that we fundraisers should

"switch our focus from monetary transactions to human connections."

This idea isn't original – and it's certainly not new. Ken Burnett introduced me to the idea with his 1992 book *Relationship*

Fundraising. Lots of very smart leaders in our sector have been talking about relationship fundraising and donor-centred fundraising for years.

I think I see the same thing that Ken Burnett saw twenty years ago. Maybe I just see it through a slightly different lens.

Switching lenses – from WHAT to WHY

We fundraisers are better at understanding behaviours than motivations.

We're great at analysis – and we've come up with many ways of defining loyal donors based on WHAT they do (which is HOW they give). "Ordinary" donors give single gifts through the mail, on the phone or via the internet. On the other hand, "loyal" donors give monthly gifts, intermediate gifts and/or legacy gifts. Knowing this is valuable – I wouldn't dare argue with that.

What I do argue though is that it's much more important to understand WHY some donors become loyal and give in these more generous ways.

The big question to Save the Pussycats is - WHY did 1,400 of their donors switch to those loyal behaviours? And WHY did the other 8,600 keep giving the regular way? What's different in the hearts, minds and souls of those loyal donors?

We can ask the same question of our triplets from earlier in the chapter. WHY did Janice give $160? And WHY did Jacqueline give more than $21,000? We know it wasn't genetics!

The most useful book I've read in the past year is called *Start with Why* by Simon Sinek. He argues that the WHY questions are always more important than the WHAT and HOW questions.

I'm completely sold on Sinek's approach – and I think it applies elegantly to philanthropy and fundraising.

Getting to the WHY of it

My answer to what separates the "loyals" from the "ordinaries" is passion. I would argue that – for the most part at least – the donors who upgraded their support to STP did so because they're passionate for both the pussycat cause and STP in particular.

Donors who step up to the plate like this do so because they're firing on all of their 3D cylinders. Their minds, hearts and souls are engaged. They've bonded. They've committed. They believe. They share strong purpose. They trust. They're loyal.

The next stop on our trip is a look at passion.

Let's go there now.

Chapter 7

The Passion Deficit

"CHASE DOWN YOUR PASSION LIKE IT'S THE LAST BUS OF
THE NIGHT."

– ANTHROPOLOGIST TERRI GUILLEMETS

In early 2009, my partners and I contracted Environics Research – a brand-name market research company – to do some polling for us on direct mail and legacy giving among adult Canadians. On a whim, we added an unrelated final question to our survey. Out of sheer curiosity, we asked 2,000 Canadian adults whether they agreed or disagreed with the statement "*I wish I had more passion in my life.*"

A majority (56%) agreed. It looks like – for the most part at least - we're a passion-hungry bunch.

This question – and the majority who responded the way they did – led to some interesting questions. What is passion anyway? Where does it fit in our lives? Why does it matter? And of course, to us at least, how does it connect to philanthropy?

Genesis of an obsession

This whole 3D Philanthropy thing started brewing in my head a year earlier - in the spring of 2008.

Springtime for me is a blur of coast-to-coast conferences and speaking gigs in April and May. It's busy and tiring – but it's also a great chance to re-connect with my fundraising friends and colleagues from across the country.

That spring, as I went from place to place, I began to notice something. When I'd ask my friends '*how are you doing?*' I got very similar answers.

"*I'm exhausted – there aren't enough hours in the day.*"

"*We're going nuts with the workload.*"

"*We're understaffed right now, and everything's way behind.*"

"*They don't pay me enough to do this.*"

I remember sitting on a plane one night, looking out over moonlit Saskatchewan. I drifted into this state where I had a little voice in each ear. One was asking '*Why is everyone so fried? Why do they seem so stressed and unhappy? What's wrong with this picture?*'

The other voice was saying, "*But this is wonderful work. We chose these jobs to be happy and fulfilled. We're saving the world and crusading for all that's good and righteous.*"

I started reflecting on the stories my colleagues had told me about how they came to work in philanthropy. They loved the causes. They loved doing good work. They wanted to surround themselves with really good people. They wanted their professional time to give their lives a deeper sense of purpose and meaning. They wanted to work in accordance with their beliefs. All noble stuff. These are motivations to celebrate.

Then, I started thinking about the people I meet on airplanes and the cab drivers I talk to. People from outside our sector. They ask me what I do for a living and I tell them. I always get the same reaction. "*That's so cool. You must love what you do. You're lucky to earn your living helping others. I'd love to do something like that.*"

People on the outside think we've got it made. That we live these enlightened and saintly lives – in the bliss and contentment of being noble people who do so much good for others.

Then I had the question that led to my own epiphany. *'Where has our passion gone? Is it dead? Or just overwhelmed? What can we do? What can I do?'*

A year later I delivered the opening plenary at the Ottawa AFP Conference – and my subject was Passion. I've been talking and writing and thinking and learning about passion ever since. I guess you could say that I've become very passionate about passion.

Oxford's got it wrong

I like to think of myself as a bit of a wordsmith. I love words. I love the way they fit together. I love knowing exactly what they mean – and learning where they come from.

One of my prized possessions is this big old Oxford dictionary I've owned since my days at St. Mary's University in the late 1970s. In the spring of 2008, I pulled that dictionary off the shelf and looked up the word "passion."

Oxford defines passion as *"a strong enthusiasm."*

Boy. What a letdown.

So, I decided to come up with my own definition. To me, passion is;

> *"an emotional and spiritual state in which we feel the joy of experiencing that which brings out the best in us."*

Our passionate moments are the ones we live for. The moments in which we feel complete and whole. The moments in which we're in the flow without effort. The moments where it just feels perfect somehow.

Let me share some of my passionate moments with you – and maybe mine will cause you to identify yours more clearly.

- I'm passionate about music. When I was younger, I used to sing with my brother's band and I used to get up and perform with the bands when I was a bartender in university. Sometimes, when you're playing music with a group of people, you all become one. You find the one groove. Everyone's in rhythm. Everyone's on key. The sounds of the different instruments almost blur into one sound. That's a beautiful moment.

- I'm passionate about nature. I remember kayaking one evening on the Mississippi River (no, not the Mark Twain one). My brother-in-law and another friend were with me, and they started fishing from their kayaks. I told them I was going to paddle upstream for awhile and that I'd be back in an hour. As I was coming back downstream I noticed some movement on the shore. I pointed myself toward the movement and sat still, letting the current take me close. It was a mother blue heron with two chicks. I'd never seen heron chicks before, so I drifted by quietly and just admired them. Then I continued to just sit and drift without paddling – and for a moment I simply became a part of everything around me. The water. The sky. The trees. I just dissolved into it all. A very zen moment indeed.

- I'm passionate about social justice. I'll never forget the day that Nelson Mandela was elected President of South Africa. His victory – to me at least – meant that anything in the world worth achieving was possible. I was elated. I was relaxed. For that moment at least, the struggle to end apartheid felt to me like it had come to a storybook ending.

There are many more. The runner's "highs" I used to experience training for a marathon when I was in grad school. Scoring the winning goal in a playoff hockey game when I was a kid. Watching my chocolate lab puppy swim for the first time. Discovering the writing of John O'Donohue. Listening to the album *Making Movies* by Dire Straits for the first time.

Passion is a high. It's a state of elevated being. You experience yourself at your best. Of losing yourself a moment. Of fleeting perfection.

Your passions are no doubt as individual as you are. Maybe you get lost in great literature or music or art. You could love movement (as I do) – dance, yoga, tai chi or snowboarding. Maybe your epicurean crank is turned by great food and wine. Or perhaps it's a Caribbean beach at sunrise or reaching a mountain's summit after a tough climb. We all have our passions. We all have our passionate fingerprints.

The German philosopher Hegel said that *"nothing great in the world has been accomplished without passion."* I think he's bang on with that observation.

Passion and the head

To me, passion transcends thinking completely. I've never thought my way into a passionate moment. Sure, I've thought about passionate experiences after the fact. I've tried to understand them and figure out how to engineer them at will.

But, it just doesn't work that way. Passion doesn't live in the head. It can't be planned and executed in a deliberate and strategic way.

The big brain is the outermost layer of our human onion. Passion comes from much deeper places.

Passion and the heart

Think back to the four primary emotions we talked about in chapter three: happiness, sadness, anger and fear. To my mind, two of these – sadness and fear – have little if any direct relationships to our passionate experiences. But, I would certainly make the case that anger and happiness do.

Most (thankfully) of my passionate moments are happy ones. Listening to or making great music. Experiencing the miracle of my natural world. Moving my body and releasing those addictive endorphins.

But, some of my passions are fuelled by anger. Many of my political and social passions are rooted in the anger I feel at the many injustices I see in the world. Poverty. Abuse. War. Violence against women. Racism. My list is pretty long.

Passion and the soul

Your soul is your passion's sweet spot.

When I think of just about any of my spiritual experiences and moments, I can link them to my passions. I think of it this way; the spiritual experience is the outcome – and the passion is the desire to have that outcome.

I have metaphysical moments in nature – so I'm passionate about kayaking and cross-country skiing. I transcend my physical self with great music and literature – so I'm passionate about making music and reading great books. I often feel this deep and instant rapport with people – and so I'm passionate about communicating and connecting. In fact, the two parts of my work that I love the most are public speaking and writing – because these actions generate those special connection moments for me.

I'll bet that if you look deeply inside yourself, you'll find that your passions are most deeply rooted in your soul. There will be emotional elements too no doubt. But you'll find their roots in your spirit. And I'd be surprised if you can really find any in that big brain of yours.

Passionate philanthropy

I'm sure you won't find it hard to make the link between your donors' passions and their philanthropic behaviours.

Let's start with the heart. People who have felt deep anger at cancer are more likely to become passionate supporters of cancer charities. People who thrill to an aria by Puccini are great candidates to become passionate donors to their local opera company.

At the soul level, it goes even deeper. Nature lovers and outdoorsy types are more likely to be passionate about their favourite environmental protection charities. People who believe deeply in one global human community can become passionate constituents of international development and human rights NGOs.

Communicating the deep human passion that you as a fundraiser share with your donors and prospects is the first step in developing the deep human bond that will generate a long-lasting and loyal relationship between you and the donor.

My passionate day with Bob Geldof

I remember that sunny summer Saturday like it was yesterday.

Normally, a beautiful weekend in July would find me outside doing something. But not this day.

On July 13, 1985 I sat glued to my TV. I was watching – and becoming a part of – a day the likes of which the world had never seen before. A day that changed my life.

What a day. What music. Mick Jagger singing *Dancing in the Streets* with David Bowie. Eric Clapton. Led Zeppelin. Queen. Paul McCartney. U2. The performances by my musical idols just went on and on – hour after hour. I was mesmerized.

At about 3 o'clock that afternoon, I went to my phone – MasterCard in hand – and called the 800-number to make my donation. It was only $25 as I recall – but that donation meant the world to me. It made me a member of the global tribe that unified around a singular purpose that day. By making that call I felt like I was doing something really important and meaningful to make my world a better place.

The magic of it was that so many rock stars had come together to mobilize people like me to support the largely-ignored global issue of famine in Africa. Two billion people in 60 countries were watching those concerts right alongside me. I felt like a part of something very, very big and very, very important. I was part of one global heart – and one worldwide soul.

That concert on that July day was the true birth of my philan-thropic soul.

Spreading the passion virus

The great thing about passion is that we can give it away without losing any of what we've got. We can share it around. Sneezing the passion virus costs us nothing – yet the person we infect with passion gets such a gift.

Think of a time when someone inspired you. When someone just seemed to lift you up to a higher plane. Maybe it was a musical performance. Or a speech. Or a novel or a movie.

I've been inspired by the oratory of Stephen Lewis and Martin Luther King Jr. I've been inspired by the wisdom of Mahatma Ghandi and Thich Nhat Hahn. I've been inspired by the writing of John O'Donohue and Henry David Thoreau. I've been inspired by the guitar playing of Eric Clapton and Mark Knopfler. My list goes on and on...

The word inspire literally means "in spirit." When we're inspired, we're elevated to a spiritual state. The soul is the nest in which inspiration hatches.

American philosopher and poet Ralph Waldo Emerson said that *"nothing great was ever achieved without great enthusiasm."* What a wonderful idea! Have you ever wondered what the word enthusiasm literally means? It means *"inspired by the presence of God."* Clearly, enthusiasm is the soul's domain.

When I was in high school, I was a jock. I played pretty much every sport - basketball and football were my passions. Despite my love for those games, I was never the best player on the team. Never the top scorer. Never the first-string quarterback. I never won an MVP award at the year-end athletic banquet.

But, I was always elected team captain. The reason? Looking back, I'm pretty sure that it was because I was the most passionate and enthusiastic player on the team. My teammates chose passion over talent in their leadership choice.

We love to be enthusiastic. We love it when others enthuse us and when we enthuse others. We love to be inspired – and we love to inspire others.

That's why the philanthropic sector is such a wonderful place to call home. It's a world full of enthusiasm. Full of inspiration. Full of passion.

Each and every one of us is blessed to do this noble work. It's just that we forget it sometimes when our heads are buried in our in-boxes.

Our 3D legacy

"ONLY PASSIONS, GREAT PASSIONS CAN ELEVATE THE SOUL TO GREAT THINGS."
    – FRENCH PHILOSOPHER AND WRITER, DENIS DIDEROT

My career has been such that I've spent much of the last decade thinking a lot about the idea of legacy. The first book I wrote was about charitable bequests – and the legacy gifts that donors leave to humanity as they exit their earthly lifetimes.

Naturally, this work has caused me to think about my own legacy. I've often asked myself *"When this lifetime of mine is over, what will it all have meant? Will my lifetime have mattered? How? To whom? Why?"*

My hope is that I'll leave a footprint on the world when I'm gone. I hope that it will be one of love and compassion. I hope that I will be remembered as thoughtful, kind, funny, enthusiastic and generous. I don't want to be remembered for achievement or success – or for money or materials.

My 3D thinking over these last months has made one thing very clear to me. Some of my own life's legacy will come from my head. Some of it will come from my heart. But most of the footprint I leave will have come from my soul. I think that's just the way of the universe.

When it's all said and done, I hope that I'll be remembered for my passion. My passion for life. My passion for the people I've loved. My passion for learning and teaching. My passion for all the good in humanity.

If I'm remembered for those parts of my soul, the trip – with all its trials and burdens – will have been well worthwhile.

Chapter 8

Once Upon a Time

When my daughter Rory was little, we shared a bedtime ritual at our house. Rory would brush her teeth and put on her pyjamas. We'd head up to her room together –and I would read – or make up – a bedtime story for her. After that, her mom would go up to kiss her goodnight and turn out the light.

Rory loved story time. Later – when she was about nine years old, I began reading her *The Hobbit* and then *Lord of the Rings* by J.R. R. Tolkein. It took us about four years to get through those books. Today, the telling of those bedtime stories is one of my fondest memories of being a dad of a little girl.

I'll never forget one of my independence milestones growing up. When I was about 8, my parents said it was okay for me to go to the library by myself. It was on the main street of Renfrew, Ontario – about eight blocks from my house.

Just after lunch on Saturdays, I'd collect the books I'd finished and walk to the library. I went myself – which was rare, since I always seemed to be with a bunch of friends any other time of the week. I'll never forget discovering Bronc Burnett. He was the fictional hero of a boy's series.

Bronc was a jock. I was a jock wannabe. (My dream was that I'd grow up to play quarterback for the Ottawa Rough Riders and left wing for the Toronto Maple Leafs.) Bronc lived in Hawaii. Each book – and there were lots in the series as I recall – was about his pursuit of some trophy. He led his middle school basketball team to the City Championship. He quarterbacked his University football team to the Rose Bowl.

Bronc was a stud. I wanted to be just like him.

I'd get home from the library, plop my books down in my room, and go out to play football or street hockey with my friends. But that night, I'd crawl under my covers and turn on my lamp – practically vibrating with excitement. I'd open the book up and settle back into my pillow. All was good with the world. Bronc and I were going on a great adventure – and it was going to last for a whole week.

Stories are 3D magic

What is it about stories?

Is there anybody on the planet who doesn't LOVE a great story? Somehow, I doubt it.

So, why do we love them so?

Storytelling is hard wired into us. Our neurological program-ming for stories goes back to my ancestors in Egypt more than 100,000 years ago. Stories were an essential ingredient in human survival.

American poet and novelist Ursula Le Guin put it very aptly:

> *"There have been great societies that did not use the wheel,*
> *but there have been no societies that did not tell stories."*

We humans have been using and loving stories for tens of thou-sands of years. The Oscars are awards for great storytelling on film. The best actor and best actress awards go to those whose characters bring those stories to life.

When I went to university in Nova Scotia, people from Cape Breton Island referred to soap operas as "the stories." Think of any joke you like: *Three Irishmen walk into a bar…*a joke is a story. When I was a kid, I was raised on the parables that Jesus told. Now, a parable is just a short story that contains some kind of moral lesson. I don't know if Jesus performed miracles. But I'm convinced that he was one of the most powerful and compelling storytellers who ever lived. And that in itself is a miracle to me.

If you phone your adult daughter (as I do) or your mom on Sunday nights – what do you do? You tell each other stories! When your kid comes home from school, you ask *"how was your day?"* If you're like me, you're not asking for a monosyllabic grunt. You're inviting a story.

You use these stories to relate to each other. To keep up with each other's lives and to share emotions attached to those stories. To **connect**.

Storytelling is the simplest way we know to connect deeply with each other – at both an emotional and soul level.

I speak at fundraising conferences all over the place. I love doing it, and I think people generally enjoy listening to what I have to say. Now, I'm a bit of a research freak. I love to fill my talks with polling stats and focus group findings. Some of these research findings are truly innovative and groundbreaking.

But, I'm often approached by people in airports. The introduction will go something like this:

> *'Hi Fraser. You probably don't remember me. My name is Linda, and I saw you speak at the AFP conference in Toronto three years ago. I just wanted to tell you how much I loved the story you told of the night your daughter was born. It made me cry because it made me remember the night I gave birth to my son.'*

So much for all that research. I have NEVER, EVER had someone approach me and tell me how impressive the research findings were.

I've given this some thought – and come up with this conclusion. I've never seen an emotional graph. I've never seen a soulful statistical table. Charts, graphs, numbers and stats are one dimensional. They speak only to the rational brain. Stories, on the other hand, are 3D magic. The human connection triple threat.

Roger C. Schank is a cognitive scientist – and a very good one at that. He's a former professor of computer science and psychology at Yale University. Currently the CEO of The Socratic Society, he's one of the world's leaders in the field of artificial intelligence. This guy knows that brain if anyone does. He says:

> *"We humans <u>are not</u> ideally set up to understand logic;*
> *we <u>are</u> ideally set up to understand stories."*

So, what makes a good story?

I'm probably not the one to instruct you on the art of storytelling.

I've never taken a course in creative writing. I've never been taught to speak in public. I know that there's such a thing as a story arc – but I couldn't for the life of me tell you what it is (unless I took a 15 minute break right now and Googled it.)

But, after some 30 years of writing and telling stories in many media, here's my handy-dandy checklist as to what makes for a good story:

- a protagonist or principal character
- a villain or enemy or problem to overcome

- a sidekick character (Batman's Robin) or perhaps a love interest (did Batman and Batgirl ever get it on?)
- some sort of quest or journey or goal to be achieved
- challenges along the way
- some sort of conflict
- the conflict comes to a climax (This is often the defining moment in a book or movie.)
- finally, a resolution or conclusion where the goal is (or isn't) reached.

So let's make up a philanthropic example and create a story sketch:

> Jason is a homeless teenager in East London. He and his best mate Andy have been making do on the streets for ten months now. Jason ran away from his parents in Sheffield because they were alcoholics and abusive to him.

> Jason dreams of being a singer. He plays his guitar (his only possession) on street corners while Andy "beats" the crowd his way.

> When Jason gets enough money in his guitar case, he and Andy go and score some crack. They get high. They come crashing down. And they head back out to play.

> One day, Jason wakes up in a hospital bed. He and Andy bought some polluted dope.

> Andy died.

> Jason has his moment of truth.

> Not long after that, a volunteer from TeenStreet drops by his room. They talk.

Jason goes to the TeenStreet Rehab Centre for a month. He joins Narcotics Anonymous. He finds a job. He stays clean for a year.

Today he's singing in a bar in Soho. He's writing material for an album. He's fallen in love. He's happy for the first time in his seventeen years on this earth.

Today, Jason is the TeenStreet volunteer who visits overdose patients in hospitals. He's come full circle.

Let's continue with developing Jason's story just a bit more.

The climax of this story – to me at least – is Jason waking up in the hospital. That's the scene (if we made the story into a movie) where we'd want to bring the moment to life. And let's look at how Jason's head, heart and soul states are jumping from one to another.

> He's lying in bed. Dazed and confused (brain). The doctor is telling him that he almost died from bad crack (fear – heart). Then, the doctor tells him that Andy didn't make it (sadness – heart).

The doctor leaves the room and Jason lies there alone. He's terrified (heart) and incredibly sad (heart) at Andy's loss. For the first time in his life, Jason feels total despair (soul). He's worthless (soul). His life has come to nothing (soul). Maybe it's time to check out of the hotel called life (soul). Jason starts to think about how he can take his own life (head).

Just then a young woman about Jason's age comes into his room (apprehension – heart). She introduces herself as Brittany – a volunteer from an organization called TeenStreet (curiosity – brain).

Brittany tells Jason about the TeenStreet Rehab Centre – where addicted youth go for addiction treatment (brain is listening and processing). She tells him that lots of young people much like him have come out of treatment and lived happy lives (combination of suspicion-heart and hope – soul).

She asks if she can come back and visit him again tomorrow. He says okay (with suspicion still in the heart and hope in the soul).

As Jason lies in silence after she's gone – he has his moment. Jason thinks back to his grade two teacher. She was the first person in his life who recognized the music in him – and told him he was special for it (worthiness – soul).

Jason bites his lip hard – and decides to fight for his life (survival – soul). He'll go to rehab and give it his best shot (determination (a form of anger) – heart). He'll do it for Andy (love – soul). But more than anything, he'll do it for himself (self love – soul).

Such a perfect fit

I'm sure you can see now why storytelling and philanthropy is such a powerful and natural fit. Great characters. Great drama. Deep emotions. Lots of soul.

I'm going to ask you to ponder an idea for a minute:

> **You're no longer just a fundraiser. From this moment on, you're a philanthropic storyteller.**

I asked for my first gift in 1980. In the three decades since, I've found that there's no more powerful way to score that gift than to tell a kickass story. Not just any story. It's got to be a story with meaning and purpose. A story with heart and soul.

Tell the right story to the right person for the right reasons – and let the magic happen.

Trust me on this one, okay?

And now - the rest of the story

Pretty much everything else to come in this book is about the pieces you can put into your stories.

- Choosing the right storytellers that give your stories a voice that's true.
- Making your story touch the heart.
- Bringing it to life by appealing to the senses.
- Stirring the soul with beliefs, meaning and purpose.
- Sticking to the stuff that's most important – the cause.
- Articulating a vision and mission that inspires and motivates the donor (rather than the ho-hum stuff on your lobby wall right now.)
- Choosing language over lingo. Expressing the beauty in the work you do.
- Staying sincere and real.

This is the mid-point of the book.

We've pretty much covered the WHY of 3D Philanthropy. Now, let's get our hands a bit dirty and learn how to actually do it.

Chapter 9

Tools for creating a 3D Connection

Up Close & Personal

The first tool in your kit is your people.

People with eyes. People with smiles. People with voices. People who bring your cause – and your organization – to life in the hearts and minds of your donors.

My case here is a simple one.

"Your messages will be received more often and more deeply if they are transmitted by real people – and not by the anonymous voice of 'the institution'."

Here's a little self-test to get you started on this chapter. I call it the real estate audit. Go to your website and look at all the space on it that's taken up by words. Of that space, how much of it contains words that are from someone specific? On the other hand, how much of your website's real estate contains words that are anonymous?

You can do the same self-test with your annual report, your donor newsletter and your organization's case for support (you have one of those, right?).

If your charity or NGO is like most, the majority of your real estate is impersonal. Most of your written real estate is institutional language that can't be tied to a face, a voice or a name.

I think this is a mistake from a 3D perspective. You see, the institution can do a pretty good job of speaking to the donor's head. The institutional voice can do a good job of articulating facts, figures, graphs and charts. But – and this is a big but! – the institution has no emotions. And it has no soul.

The three dimensional connection happens between people – and only between people. When the institution speaks too much, the 3D human connection is lost like a cell phone call with a weak signal.

Wire mommy, cloth mommy

Fifty years ago, a psychology professor named Harry Harlow performed some experiments with baby rhesus monkeys.

Soon after their births, these babies were separated from their real mothers and placed in cages with two surrogate "mothers." One of the mothers was a wire frame with a bottle full of milk. The other surrogate was also a wire frame – but this one was covered in cloth.

The baby monkeys went to the wire mothers only long enough to feed on the milk. As soon as they were done feeding, they'd rush back to the cloth mother for her warmth and softness. If the babies became frightened in their exploration of the cage, they'd rush back to the cloth mother for comfort and safety.

Harlow's research began to demonstrate just how much we need touch, connection and warm relationships in our lives. We need to comfort each other. We need to welcome each other. We need to accept each another. We need to belong with each other.

We humans are an incredibly social species. Right from the moment of birth we need to connect. When a baby is born, she is placed on her mom's breastbone. To feel warm skin. To be held in safety. To feel the pulse of her mother's heart – with which she is already very familiar.

Psychologists have demonstrated clearly that babies who start life in orphanages suffer for their lack of warm contact with mother or a mother surrogate. Infants who spend most of their time alone in cribs incur incredible risks for impaired intellectual development, behaviour problems and social problems. The cluster of issues around these babies and children is sometimes classified under the umbrella of attachment disorder. When we don't learn to attach well and securely to others, our lives becomes incredibly difficult.

We humans suffer or thrive based in large part on the nature of the relationships in our lives. Were we loved and nurtured enough by our parents? Do we share deep beliefs and values with our spouses? Do we show our children our appreciation for the miracles that they are?

This ain't new

The idea of a singular human messenger certainly isn't new. The world is full of personalities who personify organizations. My 7 year-old knows Mickey Mouse better than the Disney Brand. He also knows Michael Jordan better than he knows the Nike brand. (I find this fascinating because MJ retired from basketball a few months before my stepson Thomas was born!) Thomas is also very well acquainted with a certain clown named Ronald McDonald (much to my health food-oriented chagrin).

Tony the Tiger has been the face and the voice of Frosted Flakes for more than 50 years. Angelina Jolie is an easier connection to make than the United Nations High Commissioner for Refugees (even the acronym UNHCR is a mouthful!). Would the Muscular Dystrophy Association have raised $2.5 billion without Jerry Lewis?

The list goes on and on and on. Colonel Saunders and fried chicken. The little green gecko (who I cannot stand!) and insurance. Infomercial pitchman Vince and Sham Wow. Bono and HIV/AIDS in sub-Saharan Africa. Here in Ottawa where I live, our NHL hockey team's captain Daniel Alfredson has become an effective voice for the under the radar issue of mental health.

There's no doubt in my mind that it pays to put a human voice (or lizard's or tiger's or mouse's) voice to your organization. With the voice you acquire personality and dimension. And that, as Martha Stewart would say, is a good thing.

Quest for connection

We humans are hard-wired to connect with others. University of Chicago neuroscientist John Cacioppo has studied the physical effects of loneliness on our health. In his book *Loneliness: Human Nature and the Need for Social Connection*, he lays it out very plainly.

Fifty thousand years ago, my Egyptian ancestors depended on each other for their very survival. They shared food and warmth. They protected each other from predators and other dangers.

They shared stories that taught survival tips and skills. As a result, our brains are deeply programmed to need others in our lives.

Cacioppo demonstrates that loneliness shows up in all sorts of metrics and measurements of human health. Lonely people have elevated stress hormones, depressed immune functions and poorer cardiovascular functions. They eat more fat. They sleep poorly. They consume more alcohol. They age prematurely.

When we are too lonely, it looks to me like we go about killing ourselves. My take is that we are so social that our desire to survive is determined – at least in large part – by the value that others place in us. When others need us, we feel useful and worthwhile. And that in turn, gives purpose and meaning to our lives.

"This is why we must see fundraising and philanthropy at a much deeper level than the generation of transactions."

Your job as a fundraiser goes way beyond generating the next cheque. Your job (to me at least) is to connect with your donors at that deeply human level. To make them feel necessary and useful. To feel that they belong in your tribe. To share in your cause and your mission. To share in your beliefs and your fundamental purpose.

Acceptance, appreciation & belonging

In chapter three, we looked at the four fundamental emotions – fear, happiness, anger and sadness. I want to talk for a minute about what makes me angry.

Now, I don't think of myself as an angry guy. I have a pretty long fuse – and there are lots of days that go by in my life without many calories being burned on this emotion.

Having said that, I've come to realize that there are a few things that really light up my anger fuse.

I get angry when I feel that I'm being ignored - when I feel that someone with whom I'm in a relationship acts like I'm not there.

I get angry when I feel that I'm taken for granted, like the nights when I spend 45 minutes making dinner for my boys – and they sit down at the table and start telling me what they don't like about supper and what they'd rather have.

I get angry when I feel that I'm being bossed around. I've always been one to talk back to people in authority. Yes, I've given lip to cops who were writing up parking tickets. (Probably not the smartest thing to do, I admit.)

Where does this anger come from? I think it comes from my deep need to be accepted, to be appreciated and to be fully respected as a member of the group.

Despite my anger triggers, a psychologist would peg me as a serious people-pleaser. I want people to like me. I want them to include me. I go to great lengths to entertain, interest and engage others so that they will include me in their tribes.

We all hunger for acceptance. We all have a need to feel that we're appreciated. We all want others to respect us. But most of all, we want to be included. We need to belong.

Psychologists define three circles of human connection that contribute to strong mental, emotional and physical health.

1. We need a strong "other". That other is a parent figure when we're young. It's a best friend when we're in our teens and early adulthood. And it's a spouse or partner when we reach adulthood.

2. We need family. That intimate group of people from whom we can't hide our many flaws.

3. And we need a tribe – or community. We want to belong to a group that accepts us and with whom we strongly identify.

Solo voce

> "IF I LOOK AT THE MASS, I WILL NEVER ACT. IF I LOOK AT THE ONE, I WILL."
>
> – MOTHER THERESA

I'm afraid that I can find very little in the way of academic literature to support my claims about the power of the single voice. So I'm going to ask you to consider my opinion and make your own decision.

Having said that, Professor Paul Slovic at the University of Oregon has published some amazing findings on how we humans connect to the one rather than the many. His findings support what many fundraisers know all too well.

Slovic has studied what he calls "psychic numbing". In short, his findings go something like this: When an 18-month-old toddler named Jessica falls down and gets stuck in a well in Texas, it becomes an international news story and a media circus. A few years later, millions die in Rwandan genocide and the world turns a blind eye.

Do we ignore genocide, holocaust and mass murder because we're unfeeling and insensitive to the pain of others? Of course not. We simply absorb what our brains are able to absorb. Slovic has conducted experiments that demonstrate clearly that people respond most strongly when an issue is boiled down to one person's story.

I'll extrapolate from Slovic's theory to contend that the same works for messengers. When a message comes from one person, I understand most easily. When it comes from two people, the message begins to get fuzzy. When it comes from an institution, I simply don't relate from a heart and soul perspective. Yes, I can understand the facts, figures and logical arguments (if I'm interested that is) – but I only connect at a human level when I've got another human to connect to.

The breathing organization

Your donors and volunteers are going to connect most deeply with the PEOPLE in your organization – and not the organization itself.

Your people are going to make your donors feel appreciated. Your people will make them feel like they're an important part of the tribe. Your people are going to show them love, respect and true acceptance.

Only people can do this!

So, doesn't it make sense to focus on the people in your organization more than on the organization itself?

Think about it. Great leaders fully understand that they don't lead countries or companies or NGOs. They know that they lead people. Great managers don't manage departments. They manage people. Great coaches don't coach teams. They coach players.

It's pretty damned simple.

Who are your faces and voices?

So who are the people whose faces should be seen by your donors and prospects? Whose voices should your constituents hear?

There are a lot of them actually.

One place to start is to use the voices of other donors. They can talk about why they gave to your organization in the first place – and why they keep giving. They can talk about their connection to your cause. They can tell real stories about their lives. They can talk about shared values and beliefs. They can wear their hearts on their sleeves and talk about how they feel.

Donors are great spokespeople. So are volunteers. But, the list goes on...

Your CEO and Board Chair can speak with authority about your mission, goals and programs. They can also talk about why they've committed themselves to the cause and to your organization. They have hearts and sleeves too!

Program recipients (where appropriate) are great spokespeople. Who can better testify to the power of your program and the life-changing experience your organization brings to people?

Outside experts can offer testimonials about the credibility of your work. Employees can talk about their passion for their careers. My colleagues and I once did a fundraising letter for a hospital foundation that was signed by one of its carpenters!

Then of course, there are loved ones. Parents and grandparents can talk about their children and their experience with the cause – be it summer camp or juvenile cancer. A 50-year-old son can talk about his late mother's dedication to the local symphony. A surviving spouse can talk about her husband's dedication to Scouting.

So sit down. Make a list. Creating a spokesperson inventory is a GREAT use of your time.

An 80:20 guide

Do you remember the real estate self-test I talked about at the start of this chapter? Well, now you can start to make changes to the face your organization presents to the world.

Why not commit to an 80:20 rule?

Promise yourself that you will transform your materials – whether web site, annual report, newsletters and brochures – to the first person.

In other words, you will ensure that 80% of your organization's words are actually from somebody. Somebody real. Somebody with passion. Somebody your donor or prospect can really connect with.

Doing this well, will move you toward connecting with your donor's heart and soul dimensions – and truly bring them into your tribe.

Show me yours I'll show you mine

Once you have your inventory of spokespeople together and you start using their voices, you're halfway there. The second part of the 3D process is to have that person talk about who she really is. What she feels. Why she's involved.

Here's an example of how not to do it.

I recently made a first-time donation to a health charity. Within a week, my thank you letter and tax receipt were in my mailbox. This charity gets full marks for promptness.

The thank you letter was signed by the organization's CEO, which was fine. BUT – the CEO told me nothing about himself. No feelings. No passion. No heart. No soul. No nothing. He was just a meaningless signature at the bottom of the page.

That, from a 3D perspective, is a wasted opportunity to connect with a new donor and start a deep and longstanding relationship.

Look around your organization. Read the blurb by your Executive Director or Board Chair in your annual report. Look at your last piece of direct mail. Look at your last e-appeal. Did the person it was from show any of his or her humanity?

More often than not, this is sorely lacking in the way we talk to our donors, volunteers and friends. It's a shame, isn't it?

Collecting cause connections

Here's a simple question: Do you know which of your donors have a personal experience with your cause? If you do, you can strategically select messengers who "mirror" their connection.

Let's take the example of a prostate cancer charity. It asks its donors if they've ever been diagnosed with prostate cancer themselves, whether they've had a family member diagnosed or whether they haven't had an up-close experience with the disease.

Knowing that, the charity can choose messengers that match the donor's experience – or lack of it. We connect with people in part when we see ourselves mirrored in them.

A *thousand words*

As you begin to increase your use of real voices to speak for your organization, you should be thinking visually too. When you use a messenger in print, an accompanying photo of your messenger is a great idea – but think about how to make it the right photo.

Head and shoulder shots of your serious-looking volunteer in a business suit doesn't tell me much. Animated expression is price-less. In focus groups my colleagues and I have done, donors have a definite preference to see their dollars at work in charity pics. So, if you're a hospital foundation, a photo of a doctor in a white coat examining a patient is much better than a pic of that same doc's head and shoulders in a sports jacket and tie.

Video is a powerful connective medium. When I watch a clip, I can see the eyes, observe (subconsciously) the body language and hear the nuance in the voice. Getting your messengers up on YouTube or similar locations – and providing links from your website, is a wonderful way to create a more meaningful personal connection with your constituents.

Personal brands

Organizations have brands. Sometimes people within organiza-tions have brands too. Once in awhile the brand of the person is stronger than the brand of the larger tribe.

Tiger Woods has a bigger brand than PGA golf. Richard Branson's brand might just be bigger than Virgin's. Mickey Mouse and Disney? Colonel Sanders and KFC? I'll let you be the judge.

McDonalds Restaurants chose to use a clown named Ronald to personalize the brand. They knew that kids would identify more closely with a smiling, friendly face than with a more symbolic pair of golden arches.

A couple of years ago, we worked with an international children's charity to kick-start a bequest marketing program. This charity had been doing TV infomercials for many years – and their CEO was a familiar face with a strong reputation for integrity and compassion.

Together with this charity, we decided to send loyal donors a mail package – the centrepiece of which was a letter from the CEO. The letter would talk about his passion for the cause, his vision for the future and a story about his experience with one child who needed his charity's support.

We gathered the necessary background information and requested a short interview with the CEO so that we could capture his voice. At first the charity turned us down. "He's busy. He's out of the country. We can't do it," they said.

We persevered and finally got 20 minutes of the CEO's time. The letter that resulted captured his voice, his heart and (I think) his soul.

The response was unbelievable. Not only was the charity flooded with people telling them that a bequest was coming – but people were stopping the CEO in airports and thanking him for taking the time to write. They'd felt as though the letter was one-to-one.

There is no way that result could have been achieved without a real, authentic, honest message – reaching out from one human being to another. Nothing beats one to one.

Back to cloth mommy

"TELL ME, IN A WORLD WITHOUT PITY
DO YOU THINK WHAT I'M ASKING'S TOO MUCH
I JUST WANT SOMETHING TO HOLD ON TO
AND JUST A LITTLE OF THAT HUMAN TOUCH."
–BRUCE SPRINGSTEEN

Remember the experiment with the baby monkeys and their cloth mothers? Touch is critical to our development as infants – and it's critical to our well-being as we make our way through life.

I believe that touch extends beyond physical skin to skin contact. We touch each other with our words, our smiles and our eyes. Our gestures can make others feel accepted, appreciated and wanted. There are many ways to say to another "you belong."

I've been touched by Bob Dylan's song lyrics. By Mark Knopfler's guitar solos. By John O'Donohue's elegant writing. By the scene in the movie *Field of Dreams* where Kevin Costner plays catch with his father.

You can – and should – touch your donors in a deeply human way.

They need that touch.

Reaching out that personally is a bit scary. Take the risk. Once you get in the habit, I'm sure you'll never look back.

Chapter 10

Sincerely Yours

One Sunday morning last winter, I was driving along a country road in Lanark County. It was incredibly cold (with a wind chill of minus 39) and I'd just taken my dogs for a cross country ski. I was driving home, waiting anxiously for the car heater to kick in – and for the feeling to come back into my fingers.

I was listening to an interview with Mavis Staples on CBC Radio. Now, Mavis is one of my favourite all-time female vocalists. (If you don't know her, think of Gladys Knight without the Pips, the doo-wops and songs with pop-sounding hooks.)

Mavis started her career with the Staples Singers – a crossover gospel group that consisted of her dad (gospel music legend Pops Staples) her sisters and her brother. She went solo several years ago. Pops has now departed this earth.

She was promoting her new album – and at one point she quoted her father:

> *"What comes from the heart, reaches the heart."*

I thought that was beautifully expressed.

Then I started thinking – about the role of sincerity in philanthropy and fundraising.

It occurred to me that when we speak from the heart – and the soul – we cannot be insincere. Insincerity is entirely a product of the brain. Deep human connections then, by definition, must be sincere connections.

I then realized that we fundraisers rarely (if ever) use the word "sincerity" when we talk about our work. And yet, in my humble opinion, there's nothing more important to our success.

Donors and prospects need to know us fully. They need to share with us – whether they share our beliefs, our sense of purpose or the value we place on your organization's mission. That sharing leads to trust – which in turn leads to loyalty.

And loyalty, my friends, leads to a much-improved bottom line for your organization.

Let's try to define exactly what we mean by the word sincere. To me, the notion of sincerity has two important elements:

1. Something is sincere if it is absolutely truthful, AND

2. If what's said is done so without any guile, manipulation or spin.

Let me give you an example:

> Many years ago, I was driving aimlessly through Tennessee. I ended up in Memphis and couldn't resist a visit to Graceland (even though I've NEVER been an Elvis fan!). We were touring the Elvis Museum and the tour guide was pointing out Elvis' various onstage outfits.
>
> Being the smarty-pants that I am, I asked her (in front of a group of about 20 diehard fans) *"Just how much did Elvis weigh when he died?"*
>
> She replied *"Many people are surprised to learn that Elvis was actually quite a tall man. He stood six feet and three quarters of an inch tall."*
>
> Was she truthful? Absolutely.
> Was she being sincere? No way.

I'm convinced that donors today are savvy, sophisticated and wary. They're sick of the tricks of the trade. They know B.S. when they hear it – and they just want the straight goods. So how can you be sincere with your donors in a way that will build trust and loyalty?

Beyond truthfulness and lack of spin, I think there's one more aspect to sincerity. When we're sincere, we're vulnerable. We don't try to patch over our cracks and flaws. We present ourselves as we truly are.

There's a conundrum here. On the one hand, we've had a lot of our sincerity "taught out of us" – probably by parents and teachers. On the other hand, we absolutely love it when others show their vulnerability to us.

Showing vulnerability involves risk. And that risk involves fear. Fear is a powerful emotion that protects our ability to survive.

Courage is acting in the face of fear. So, showing vulnerability and sincerity requires you to be brave. I'm asking you to suck it up like a good soldier and do it. Open yourself to criticism and possible attack – because along with that risk comes incredible embrace.

Here are five thoughts/ideas to help you get started on your own sincerity program:

1. Try never to speak with the institution's voice – because in truth, the institution doesn't actually have a voice. Your messages should be from real people (your leaders) to real people (your donors). It's all about human connections isn't it?

2. Your spokesperson or ambassador should show all three of her dimensions. She should speak with her head, her heart and her soul. This means that she must open up and show some of her real self. I can tell you right now that your donors will love this – but the

people you're asking to speak this way will resist you (at least in the beginning).

3. Pay particular attention to how you say thanks to your donors. I recently received a thank you letter from the CEO of one of Canada's biggest health charities. The first sentence started "Please accept my heartfelt thanks..." But that's all it said. Guess what? It backfired. Rather than making me feel connected, I felt like I was being patronized. The thank you didn't go far enough or deep enough to feel real and human to me.

4. Admit your flaws. Go ahead! Tell your donors that you're not perfect. Tell them immediately when you screw up and make mistakes. Tell them when you're struggling. I forced myself to take this approach early on in my fundraising career – and it's always paid big dividends. People appreciate honesty – and the expression of a sincere desire to fix mistakes and do better next time. (Thanks for the lesson mom!)

5. Always start with WHY. Why does your organization do the work it does? Why do your board members volunteer? Why should donors give to you – and not the other 160,000 organizations in Canada who also want their attention and money? Answering the WHY questions well always gets to the heart of the matter. That's why it's the perennial favourite question of every two- and three-year-old I've ever met!

Sincere people don't use manufactured language. Let me give you an example:

Not long ago, I reviewed some fundraising and marketing materials for a hospital foundation in Western Canada. One of the donor reports had the title *Enhancing Patient Care*. As soon as I read those three words, I could feel myself turning off. I now had to force myself to read the rest of the report. That simple phrase had turned my reading into work.

When I discussed the report with the client, we talked about other ideas. We talked about people helping people. About being there for neighbours and friends. Real stuff, instead of manufactured slogans. She agreed to change the title page into something more human – and to me, sincere.

There's no question in my mind that sincerity is a critical element of 3D communication.

"If we want to connect with our minds, hearts and souls, we can't afford to use jargon and empty slogans. We simply say what we mean – and mean what we say."

In my experience, people always respect and appreciate sincerity. If your organization is rigorous in creating a culture of sincerity, you'll soon find that your efforts are richly rewarded by more loyal donors and greater revenue.

Chapter 11

Triggering Emotions

> *"Emotions aren't always*
> *immediately subject to reason,*
> *but they are always immediately subject to action"*
> —William James

Let's start the presentation of this tool by doing a quick review of what we discussed in Chapter 3 – The Heart.

Our emotions (the second dimension in 3D Philanthropy) are hard-wired into us. The emotions I'll experience today were programmed by my Egyptian ancestors more than 100,000 years ago.

Emotional combustion takes place in the old brain – a.k.a. the limbic system. Our emotions are primal, very strong at times and have no language. They simply fire into our systems – often without warning – and if their charge is strong enough, dominate any thinking we may be doing at the time.

Darwin was right

Our emotions are there because they served an incredibly important purpose for tens of thousands of years. In short, they were key to our survival.

- Your ancestor feared the tiger and ran away before becoming his dinner – and you're here today as a result!

- He got angry when the caveman from down the path leered at his wife. So he punched the neighbour in the jaw and sent him packing. That's why he's your ancestor – and not the creepy neighbour.

- He felt incredible sadness when his wife fell into the river and drowned. He swore he wouldn't feel that way again – and was much more attentive to his next wife. So, here you are.

- Having his first daughter made him incredibly happy. His joy at fatherhood made him want more children. The third of those children led through the generations to you.

You and I wouldn't be here – our species wouldn't be here – without human emotions. Our emotions have served humanity well for the past hundred millennia. We're still here, aren't we?

The turbo effect

It's critical to understand that when we're experiencing a strong emotion, our brain takes the back seat.

"The heart trumps the brain"

– pretty much every time. Think of the last time you lost it with one of your kids (or your mother or your partner). Were you thinking clearly? Were you deliberately trying to achieve a productive outcome? Were you being strategic?

Nope. You were just letting fly your frustration. You probably did more harm than good. But, once that angry outburst started, you couldn't hold it back if you wanted to.

The compass of the heart

In Chapter 3, we looked at the four primary emotions; fear, anger, happiness and sadness. Let's go a bit deeper with that palette now.

Picture a compass – with the four primary emotions being the four directions; north is fear, south is anger, east is sadness and west is happiness. Sketch it out on a piece of paper if it helps.

Go from the centre (your heart) to one of the four points. Now keep going.

As you pass that 'primary point' (let's say fear) your pencil starts making branches – like those on a tree. One of the four fundamental emotions splits off into many, more specific, sub-emotions.

Here's what I mean:

- Fear leads to: anxiety, shyness, embarrassment, confusion, worry and jealousy.

- Sadness leads to: guilt, regret, loneliness, depression, alienation, apathy, boredom, disappointment, discouragement and regret.

- Happiness leads to: pride, ecstasy, excitement, enthusiasm (which, to me is also a spiritual state), hope, optimism, infatuation, relief, gratitude, satisfaction, bliss and mischievousness.

- Anger leads to: frustration, impatience (a personal favourite of mine!), annoyance, stubbornness, disgust, envy, aggression and exasperation.

This list is by no means complete. And, in the research I've done, there is certainly no consensus among the experts as to *the* definitive list of emotions we carry in our portfolios. But I hope you get the idea.

Philanthropy with heart

So how does emotional intelligence make you a better fundraiser? Let's get down to business.

Going to the emotions zone with your donors is a pure play for a heart connection. The mind doesn't connect with emotions. Nor does the soul.

"The singular most powerful way for you to connect with another is at the level of heart and feelings."

First off, I want to argue with a conventional wisdom that pervades our profession. That wisdom is that donors give initially from an emotional impulse – but that as they continue to give (and give more) their focus shifts from emotional to intellectual considerations.

Now, I'm not dismissing the intellectual part. But I fundamentally disagree with the idea that at some point in the relationship, your donor starts acting solely in response to his or her brain. Human beings just don't behave that way – at least in my experience.

The primary question I'd like you to operate from is "how can I help my donor get into the right emotional state to maximize the likelihood of a gift and the size of gift I want to ask her for?"

There are three simple ways in which you can get started with this:

- **Ask** the donor how she feels about a situation or an experience – or how she would feel if she were in a certain situation.

- **Tell** stories with characters that are explicit about their feelings. Those characters can be your volunteers, your program staff – and of course the people who are the recipients of your programs or services.

- **Talk** about your own feelings!

Let's create an example of how we touch the four compass points in one communications piece. Let's say we're a hospital foundation, and we want to do an article from a doctor who does complex heart surgeries.

We decide that we'll write this piece under his by-line. So, in the first person, he tells us a story about his work.

- After giving us a bit of background about his area of specialty and some context on the state of cardiology in Canada today, he introduces us to a 68-year-old man who needs a complex – and somewhat risky – operation to save his life.

- The surgeon describes the first meeting with the man and his wife. The man seems angry that this has happened to him, because he's always exercised, refrained from smoking and stuck to a healthy diet. The doc explains that some heart conditions are the luck of the gene pool, but the patient is still upset.

- As the couple leave his office, the doctor recalls a patient who had the same procedure last month. This patient developed complications and died two weeks later. The doc recalls how sad he felt when he learned of his patient's death. The two of them had connected really well personally – and the surgeon felt the loss deeply.

- On the morning of the surgery, the doc drops by his patient's room for a final check in. The patient's wife is sitting in a bedside chair, trying so hard to be cheerful and brave. But her lip is quivering and she's dabbing small tears from the corners of her eyes. It's clear that she's terrified at the prospect that she might lose her husband.

- The three-hour procedure is finished and the surgeon goes to the waiting room to tell the patient's wife that everything went well. She beams with joy and practically jumps into the doctors' arms as she says thank you over and over again.

There you have it. A compass point story. The angry patient at the consult. The doctor's sadness at recalling a patient who didn't make it. The wife's fear before the operation – and her incredible happiness when she found out it had all gone well.

This ain't rocket science. But when a well-told story covers some or all of the compass points, it's powerful to the person hearing it. Why? Because, in some way, shape or form, we've all been there.

In doing this, you achieve a couple of things. First, the donor who opens up emotionally experiences a certain catharsis. A release or cleansing of sorts. A relieving of some pressure inside. This is followed by a feeling of relief and peace.

Secondly, the donor innately feels closer to you when emotions are opened up and allowed to run. A certain intimacy is created. The seeds of trust are planted. And trust is a critical element of loyalty. At the end of the day, 3D Philanthropy is all about creating greater donor loyalty – and greater revenue as a result of that loyalty.

Emotional to-do list

If I was asked to come to your organization, do an emotional audit and make some emotionally-based recommendations, here's a list of a half-dozen practical ways in which you could increase your EQ.

1. The Executive Director's message at the front of your annual report would have him express how he feels about his work. Why he loves his job. Why he took the job in the first place. How he feels when the organization succeeds – and when it comes up short.

"I'll never forget that trip I took to India in 1983. I had just graduated from university, and I wanted to travel before getting tied down to a career. In many ways that trip was a better education than I'd had during four years at McGill. I saw people who lived in tiny shacks. They were so thin. There were so many children. They had next to nothing. Yet, there was something in their eyes – and in their smiles. They were members of my family. They were me. When I came home, I decided not to pursue engineering with a major North American firm. Rather, I decided to look for a NGO that could use my skills to help build communities in which people could be productive and happy. Today – almost thirty years later – I've never regretted that decision. My career has given me a peace and contentment I didn't know was possible. I'm excited to go to work on Monday morning. I relish each and every day of giving and receiving the means of building true happiness."

2. I'd have a story appear front and centre on your web site's home page. It could be text or it could be (better if you can do it well) video. The narrative is about a person who's received your program or service. How her life has changed. And – most importantly – how she FEELS now that those changes have happened.

"Ever since I was a little girl, I dreamed of being a nurse. But growing up in social housing – with my mom on social assistance – I realized as I got older that nursing would always just be a dream for me. I used to feel sad thinking that I would never walk down a hospital corridor with that name badge around my neck. I worried about what I'd be able to do without a college or university education. In my life, I've spent a lot of time feeling fear about my future. But now, thanks to the Anybody Can Scholarship Fund, that's all changed. I've applied to nursing school – and with my marks, I think I'll be accepted. I'm so excited to start learning – and to finally meet others who have the same dream as me.

3. I'd recommend that your thank you letter to first-time donors show the person behind the signature at the bottom – and show how that signatory really feels about the cause and the organization.

"I first became a supporter of the Learning Disabilities Association when my daughter was in the third grade. She would sit at the dining room table after supper – struggling with her spelling homework. She would burst into tears and say, 'Dad, I just can't do this. There's something wrong with my brain.'

Those words broke my heart. But, as any good father would do, I became determined to find a way to help her overcome her incredible frustration and feelings of failure. I called LDA – and learned about different ways in which I could help her to learn to spell – ways that worked with (rather than against) her brain. Today, a decade later, I'm the Chair of the Board of Directors. I feel an obligation to help every kid I can. You must feel some of that obligation too – and for that I thank you. Your kindness and generosity will help us take that fear and frustration away from more children. For that, I feel very grateful to you."

4. Great major gift fundraisers are (to me at least) really good at two things. They ask great questions. And they listen incredibly well. So, a major gift fundraiser for a hospital foundation might ask a prospect:

"Do you remember the first time you were a patient with us? What was it like?"

"How did you feel when they came in to prep you for the operation?"

"Tell me what the surgeon said when he came out to tell you about Harry's bypass."

"What did it mean to you to know that your husband was going to be okay?"

"That happened six years ago now. When you think back, how do you feel about it today?"

You get the idea.

5. My colleagues and I are obsessive about interviewing people whose voices will represent the organization. I recommend that you interview those "voices" with as much time, energy and determination as you will invest in the product – be it on paper, a live speech or video presentation. Use the interview to ask the "feelings questions". In my experience, people in the social services and international development sectors tend to go to their feelings more easily. Doctors and academics are tougher nuts to crack – but that doesn't mean you shouldn't keep trying.

    "During the surgery, I was focussed on perfect technique. I was in pure technical mode - doing each step as carefully and deliberately as I could. When the tiniest mistake can mean the death of a patient, I can't afford to be any other way.

    But as I walked down the corridor afterward to talk with his wife, I came back to the bigger picture. That man on my table was a husband, a father and a grandfather. He has so much to live for. As I turned the corner and saw her, I felt a pride and joy in what I'd just done. I felt a deep gratitude that I'd been given this opportunity to heal people in need. In that moment, I felt like the luckiest man on earth."

6. Another thing my colleagues and I often encourage our clients to do is to ask donors to share their own stories and feelings. In thank-you notes. On the web site. Talking to them on the phone.

    When a donor shares her story, she's taking a step of trust. And often, you find something powerful that you can share with other donors to help build their connection with you – and their loyalty to you.

    "Please accept my donation of $200 to help the people in Bangladesh you talked about in your letter. In 1946, my brothers and I were refugees in Austria. The war had just ended – and our lives had been obliterated during the War. Our parents were dead. Our home was bombed to rubble. We had no money. We had no food. We had no place to sleep.

For two years, we survived on CARE packages. Tinned food. Pants and shirts. Blankets .Toothbrushes. People in North America were helping us when we had no other way to help ourselves.

That was more than fifty years ago. But over those fifty years, I've never forgotten the kindness of strangers. I've never lost my sense of gratitude and blessing. I have given back to CARE Canada since I moved here in 1958 – and I will continue to give as much as I'm able until the day I die. Thank you for what you did for my brothers and me. Thank you for what you do for everyone who needs help so desperately."

Some final thoughts...

I encourage you to create your own emotional compass. Start with the four primary emotions – and then add their derivatives over time. Keep your map posted somewhere in your workplace – or even make it your computer wallpaper for a few months.

Remember that behaviour change takes time. Old habits have deep grooves and new habits have to overcome them. It's a big job. Be patient – but stick with it.

When you start expressing your organization in more emotional terms you may receive different types of response within your organization. Some people will love it (I hope!). Others aren't going to like it. It'll make them feel as uncomfortable as a tight pair of shoes. They'll resist. They'll give you reasons why it isn't right to be so open and vulnerable. Changing organizational culture is one of the most difficult things we can undertake to do. But most important things are tough.

On the other hand, I can pretty much guarantee that your donors, volunteers and constituents will love the new approach. Take your strength from them. Because at the end of the day, they're the ones who really matter.

Good luck with it!

Chapter 12

Sensual Philanthropy

Donor Dossier

Name:	Wilf (remember him?)
Age:	62
Marital Status:	Divorced
Profession:	high school music teacher
Children:	two adult daughters, one adult son
Religion:	Roman Catholic
Passions:	classical music (especially Baroque), reading, foreign films

One of the best tools available to deepen your human level of communication is the explicit appeal to the senses. Sensory narrative of any kind – whether written or oral – transcends the thinking brain and brings the other in the relationship to the emotional or the spiritual plane.

Looking back, I suspect that I first learned the true power of sensual communication from my mom in the 1970s.

It was my first year at St. Mary's University in Halifax. I'd chosen to go to school a long way from my home in Ottawa. I was ready for independence. To strike out on my own.

During my first year, my mom would write to me every week (a practice I later adopted when my own daughter chose to attend the University of British Columbia).

She would always write to me on Sunday afternoon – and I would usually receive her letter late that week. She would write about family and neighbourhood events in her vivid and detailed style. She was very good at bringing me into the moments she described. Her letters always made me feel like I was there.

My mom always ended her letters in the same way – describing what the family was going to have for Sunday dinner.

> *"Well sweetie, I should go now. I can tell by the smells wafting from the kitchen that the roast beef and Yorkshire puddings are done. Just know that when we sit down for dinner we'll all be thinking about you."*

I loved life in university residence. I made a lot of friends and had lots to do. But, in those days, residence cafeteria food REALLY sucked. On Sundays I'd head down for dinner and get a plate of greyish meat, nondescript mashed potatoes and vegetables so overcooked you could just swallow them without chewing.

I'd sit down, look at that plate, and think of my mom's letter. Then I'd feel a little sad and lonely. At that moment every Sunday, a part of me wished I was back home.

My mom knew exactly what she was doing!

Let's take a look at Wilf's sensual highlights as he makes his way through his work day...

- On his way to work, Wilf stops at The Equator Roasting Company – an independent coffee house that sells coffee beans, coffee and espresso drinks. Now, Wilf has loved coffee since his university days, and he has developed quite a taste for the stuff. He can talk about coffee the way a sommelier talks about wine.

Wilf says hi to the young woman behind the counter and orders his favourite – a large Yirgacheffe dark roast. When he gets his coffee, he steps outside onto the sidewalk and takes his first sip.

Ahhh....

The taste is earthy, deep and a little bitter. He closes his eyes for a moment and almost meditates on his tongue and the roof of his mouth. He smiles a tiny smile, reaches into his pocket for his car keys and heads back into his commute. A little happier. A little more satisfied.

- When he gets to the school, he heads to his classroom and reaches into the top drawer of his desk. He takes out his baton. Wilf conducts the grade 7-8 band – and he's just had an idea for a new piece he thinks they can learn.

Wilf gazes at the back wall of the classroom and begins to conduct his imaginary orchestra. Wilf's baton is like an old friend. It was a university graduation gift – and he's had it for 22 years now. It's slender, smooth and light. It feels like it comes to life in his fingertips. Wilf loves the feel of that baton. It fits him perfectly.

- On his way home, Wilf makes his weekly stop at HMV. He goes straight to the classical section and begins to browse. On Monday, he read a great review of a recording of Bach's *Brandenburg Concertos* with Trevor Pinnock conducting. He's dying to hear it.

There it is. Wilf buys it immediately and pops the CD into his car in the parking lot. As the first few bars of the overture hit him, Wilf feels downright blissful. He's loved these concertos since high school – and this recording is particularly fine. The drive home is smooth and seamless. Wilf is lost in his music.

- When he gets home, he opens his back door and steps into his kitchen. He's immediately enveloped in the warm embrace of the smell of chicken and dumplings. He'd set up his slow cooker earlier this morning – and now his dinner is ready.

  Chicken and dumplings has always been Wilf's favourite meal – his comfort food. When he was a kid, he fell in love with them – and he still uses his mom's recipe to this day. Wilf takes a deep inhale through his nostrils and savours the smell. He breathes out slowly, and his shoulders immediately relax.

- Later that evening, Wilf takes his dog out for their evening walk. He's crossing through the neighbourhood park when he looks up and stops in his tracks. The sunset tonight is magnificent.

  The sun has half dropped below the horizon. It's a deep red-orange – and the sky around it is a combination of purple, deep blue and pink. Thin white and grey clouds have been sketched over the colour palette. Wilf pauses and admires the sight. After a moment, he gives the leash a little tug and the two of them continue on their way.

These moments are but a handful of the sensual moments Wilf has had on this day. The moments involving his five senses – sight, sound, taste, feel and smell.

As fundraisers, we don't often think specifically about our senses – or our donors' senses. But we should. Our senses are the five channels through which the world comes to us. All of our experiences – all of our memories – are rooted in our senses.

If you stop and think about it, many of your childhood memories are specifically linked to your senses. The smell of your mom's cooking. The sound of your skates on the ice in winter. You get the idea.

The word sensual means *"connected to or pertaining to the senses."* The senses – in my humble opinion at least – are a huge factor in the donor's gift decision. They provide the raw data upon which the donor makes her decision to give or not to give.

Let's look at some more sensual examples that are immediately connected to philanthropy.

- My colleagues and I once wrote some fundraising material on behalf of an international relief and development NGO. As part of our background preparation, we interviewed a Canadian aid worker who had just returned from a refugee camp in Darfur, Sudan.

  We were asking her about conditions in the camp – and how donated dollars were helping the displaced people who were living there. At one point, she began to describe the sound of a starving baby's cry. She described it as faint and coming from the top of the throat – as opposed to the diaphragm. She said it sounded nothing like the cry we know from our experience with our own babies. She went on to tell us that babies cry like this to soothe their own pain as they endure their last hours on this earth.

  Even though I had never heard that cry myself, the ear inside my head could imagine it from her description. It was very real. Quietly powerful. And very, very sad and tragic.

  By describing that sound to the NGO's donors, we were able to bring them into that camp. Seat them right down beside that poor baby. Let them share in that terrible moment. Experience the tragedy for themselves.

- A friend and colleague of mine is a former Director of Development at a Jewish Long-Term Care facility. I remember her telling me once how she'd come up with a great way to cultivate major gifts prospects and donors before making her ask.

She would invite the prospect to come for a visit and a tour of the residence. And, she'd time the visit for the hour before lunch or dinnertime. During the tour, she would take the donor through the dining room. It would be filled with the smells of traditional Jewish food. More often than not, the donor would take a big whiff and say something like "That smells just like my grandma's kitchen. When I was a kid, we always went to grandma's for dinner on the Sabbath." My friend always found it easier to close a gift after the donor had remembered grandma's kitchen.

(By the way, although smell (along with taste) is in my experience the most difficult sense to communicate to donors, remember this. Our sense of smell is most strongly linked to memory. That's why the dining room cultivation move works so well.)

- Several years ago, one of my colleagues interviewed a world-renowned heart surgeon to prepare for some writing we were going to do on the foundation that raised money on the institution's behalf.

 At one point, she asked the surgeon this brilliant question: "What does it actually feel like to hold a beating human heart in your hand?"

At first, the doctor described the physical sensations of doing heart surgery; the feel of a beating, slippery grapefruit-sized muscle as his fingers navigated the way through its chambers and arteries.

But then he shifted gears – and began to talk about the tremendous responsibility he feels when doing his operations. He said that somehow it didn't feel right that he should have this God-like power over the life and death of another. That he wasn't worthy of that duty. Yet, he knew in his mind that if he didn't do the surgery the patient would likely die.

Pretty profound and existential stuff. And it all started with the question - "What does it feel like?"

- In the part of Canada where I live there's a famous philanthropist named Ryan Hreljac. He's been a well-known humanitarian for more than a decade. At the time I'm writing this, Ryan is all of twenty years old.

Ryan first learned about the problem of unsafe and unhealthy water in the developing world when he was in his first grade classroom. He immediately set about raising money to help. Shortly thereafter, Ryan's first well was dug in northern Uganda. Ryann continued his fundraising – and eventually a foundation was formed in his name. Today, Ryan's Well Foundation has finished more than six hundred water projects that have allowed more than 700,000 people to live healthier lives.

Last summer, my wife and I were surfing the TV before bedtime. We came across a documentary on Ryan and decided to watch it. There was a segment of the program where Ryan and his parents went to Uganda to officially open one of the wells he had funded. This little kid (I'm guessing he was about 9 years old at the time) was treated like a foreign head of state in the village. The camera followed Ryan as he walked with local women and children to the pond where they used to get their water. The women and kids all had plastic buckets and jerry cans. The pond, once they got there, was a kind of yellow-brown with lots of unidentifiable stuff floating in it.

Then, the camera cut to the well in the middle of the village. A man began cranking the pump-handle and before long this perfectly clear gush of water emerged. Ryan knelt down, cupped his hands and drank from the well. He looked up, grinned and exclaimed that the water tasted great!

As I watched, I could imagine the taste of that pond water in my mouth – and my hesitation before swallowing it. I could also taste that cool well water and imagine gulping it down under the midday Ugandan sun. That documentary did its job. I shared the experience at a sensory level.

- I'll never forget the morning I dropped in to visit a friend and colleague, The Reverend Stirling Irvine. Sterling was, among other things, the Executive Director of a charity called Operation Go Home. This organization worked with downtown city street kids – offering a range of programs and services designed to help them cope on the streets, get off the streets and ultimately (if appropriate) re-unite with their families.

  I sat down in his office and noticed a poster on the wall. The poster consisted of a photo and a caption below it. The photo was of a beautiful one-year-old baby girl. She was sitting on the floor, wearing only her diaper. She was fair-skinned with fine blonde hair. Her skin was pale but her cheeks were very rosy. And, she had the biggest, most adorable blue eyes you could imagine.

  But – the baby was wearing heavy makeup. She had on dangling ear rings. She had on a deep crimson lipstick.

  The caption below the photo read *"Prostitutes aren't born. They're made."*

  That image – and those words – bored a deep hole into my brain. Several times over the years I've gone back to that office and every time I'm transfixed by that poster. The image is disturbing and unforgettable.

  It's a case statement in five words. Brilliant. Sometimes a picture is indeed worth a thousand words.

So now, let's bring it back to you; your cause, your organization. What are the sensory thoughts and images you can communicate to bring your donors to a deeper level of human connection?

Some are no-brainers. Many environmental organizations use great visual images to depict their work. Charities involved in the performing arts can utilize audio and or visual messages to bring their missions and programs to life.

But if we think a little harder we can come up with more creative ideas. A food bank could describe the taste of a dinner being enjoyed by a less fortunate child. An animal protection charity could describe the smell of an abused pet that had just come into its care. A breast cancer survivor could describe the first time she ran her fingertip along the scar left by her surgery.

You should be able to find the two senses that best fit your cause, mission and program. Find them. And then, figure out how to express them to your donors in ways that will make them think. Make them feel. Make them connect with their souls.

When I started taking golf lessons about fifteen years ago, my teacher first spent some time with me trying to figure out my learning style. I was unfamiliar with the concept, so I asked him about it. He explained to me that everybody has a dominant "style" of learning – visual, auditory or tactile. Some of us think and learn most easily and naturally in pictures and images. Some of us learn best in sounds - and still others by touch or feel.

After some experimentation, he came to the conclusion that I'm an auditory learner – so he concentrated on explaining golf swing concepts to me, more so than showing me or having me "feel" them by trying things myself.

I've later confirmed that I am indeed very much an auditory learner. If I pull up your phone number from my memory, I hear myself reciting it. I don't see it. I learned after much trial and error with second grade spelling practice that my daughter has inherited this trait from me big-time.

So, when you're communicating a message to someone else, think about the fact that she might very well have a different processing style than you do.

Here's a great exercise to finish up on sensual philanthropy:

Think of a story that illustrates your cause and your organization really well. Then, write it, incorporating all five of the senses. Approaching your story this way will help you begin to develop some "sensual discipline".

I'll take a stab at an example:

> A few hours after her surgery, Janet began to stir in her hospital bed. Slowly, she opened her eyes. Everything was quite blurry at first, but soon she was able to make out someone cleaning the floor in the hall outside her door. The light from the open window hurt her eyes a little.
>
> Janet inhaled and noticed the antiseptic smell of the floor cleaner the janitor was using. It reminded her of the stuff her janitor used in the hallways way back in public school. She could faintly hear a radio playing. The song was *Mandy* by Barry Manilow. Janet always hated that song.
>
> Then she remembered where she was and why she was lying in that bed. Janet immediately felt a jolt of fear and anxiety as it all came back to her.
>
> Slowly she reached under her nightgown and began to run her fingertips over the left side of her chest. Where her breast had been yesterday, there was only the rough ridge of what must be her surgical scar.
>
> Janet began to choke on something thick and salty. She only then realized that she'd started to weep.

Expressing the sensory nature of your work is not always easy and obvious. It takes effort and imagination. But if your goal is to transcend the brain connection with your donors and reach their hearts and souls, it's well worth the effort.

Chapter 13

Purpose and Meaning

"CHALLENGING THE MEANING OF LIFE IS THE TRUEST EXPRESSION OF THE STATE OF BEING HUMAN."

— VICTOR FRANKL

My stepson Zachary is sixteen. He's an incredibly gifted young man – with an IQ that's off the chart. In many ways, I think he's an old soul. He can converse, debate and discuss topics that most people his age can't even name. He has a beautiful mind.

Sometimes, Big Zee and I engage in quite philosophical discussions. But when we get to anything related to existentialism (the "why am I here question", he gets – umm – flustered). Zachary knows he wants to get a great education. He wants a very comfortable material life. He wants to be happy. But that – from what I've heard so far at least – seems to be as far as it goes.

In my opinion, Zachary hasn't figured out why he's here. He hasn't affixed a meaning to his life. He doesn't yet have purpose.

This doesn't surprise me. Very few of the sixteen-year-olds you see at the mall have any kind of clue as to what their lives mean. Fewer still have purpose.

Zachary's lack of meaning and purpose doesn't really concern me at all. He's young. It will come. To quote the Bible, "To everything there is a season, and a purpose under Heaven." Zee's season will come in time.

Barb's chakras & my midlife crisis

My friend Barb is 43 years old. We share interests in our work –
and in the Japanese energy healing tradition of Reiki. We talked
on the phone not long ago. When I asked how she was doing she
said, *"I'm feeling kind of messed up. My chakras are way out of balance
or something. I don't know what's going on with me."*

A little later in the conversation she told me that her dad had
passed away a few months ago. He'd been quite sick for some
time. Barb and her dad had always been very close.

Then it hit me.

When I was the same age, I felt that way too. I lost my mom when
I was 44. My mom and I shared some incredible kind of wave-
length. We simply understood each other very easily. Losing her
sent me into a tailspin.

I remember those mornings like they were yesterday. I'd get up at
5 a.m. Go downstairs and make coffee. Then go out onto my patio
and sit on this bench with my back to the clematis on the lattice
fence. I'd watch the sun rise and ask myself the same questions -
over and over. Morning after morning.

*"Am I happy? How much time do I have left? What should I do with
the time I have left? What needs to change? What does all this* (not
really sure what 'this'meant) *mean?*

Why. Am. I. Here?"

My mom's death triggered my existential crisis. At the midway
point in my life (give or take) I was questioning everything.
Suddenly it became important to me that what I did mattered. I
had this scarce thing called time – and this precious thing called

life. Suddenly, they were treasures to me – and the last thing I wanted to do was squander them.

I guess I'm describing what some people call a mid-life crisis. To me, mid-life describes *when* it happens. The more important questions (in my opinion at least) are *what* it is – and *why* we must go through it.

Ten years back – and twelve years ahead

Now, let me turn the clock back ten years. I was 34 years old and living in Toronto. I had been married for four years – and had a one-year-old daughter. I had just been promoted to a very senior position in my political career – and had become a player in my Party's upper echelon.

Back then, I was brimming with confidence – and charging forward. Life had no limits. I was getting traction under my feet. I was finding my groove – and was doing really well.

I thought I had my existential questions well in order. I was in politics to save the world from the bad greedy guys. I'd started my family. I was following my script.

Now, let me jump forward to today.

Twelve years after my mom's death, my questions have (for the most part) been answered. I'm more comfortable in my own skin than I've ever been. I've looked deeply into the mirror and really gotten to know the guy inside it. I found my soul mate – and married her at the age of 54. I've struggled with my demons and cast many of them out.

My daughter – who was in diapers when I was 34 – is a grown woman now. I've taken two stepsons into my life and my heart.

When I talk to Zachary about 'life stuff', I'm coming from a much clearer and more coherent place than I would have been when Rory was his age.

Existential answers

So where has my existential struggle delivered me?

I think I now have answers on a few levels:

- My career calling is to empower people to connect more deeply with others. The three things I love most about my work are thinking through how to do it as well as I can, public speaking and leading workshops (where I can see their eyes, as people have their aha moments) and writing. My calling told me that I must write this book. It's not all that important to me how many people read it – or how much they like it. What IS important to me is that I say it – and give people the chance to learn something from it.

- My life's purpose is threefold:

  - To find peace. By peace, I don't mean ending violence (which of course, I would love to see). I mean peace within myself. Accepting myself despite my many shortcomings. Believing that I'm worthy without having to be perfect. Actually loving myself for who I am – and letting go of who I think I should be.

  - To find wisdom. To me, knowledge is all the stuff you know – while wisdom is understanding what matters. I've had many guides in this search. Ghandi. Buddhist wise guy Thich Nhat Hahn. Irish writer and mystic John O'Donohue. My mom and my wife. The list goes on – and I won't bore you with all of it.

  - And last but not least, to give and receive all the love I can. John Lennon nailed it when he wrote "all you need is love, love – love is all you need." Learning to love well – especially learning to love myself – is probably the toughest thing I've ever tried to do. But each step toward that destination makes me appreciate how love and life are really one and the same.

- My spiritual purpose is to elevate my being to a higher plane. A finer frequency. To advance my karma – and to do what I can to help advance the karma of those around me. To shed some of the weight of this world and be more attuned to the next one (what you might call heaven, nirvana or rebirth).

With apologies to Erik Erikson

German psychologist and psychoanalyst Eric Erikson is known for developing his "eight-stage theory of human development." (If you're not familiar with it, I recommend that you check it out.)

So, with apologies to Erikson, I'd like to offer my take on our development with respect to the issue of life's purpose and meaning. To my mind, there are three stages:

1. **No problemo**: During the first third to half of our lives, we journey merrily along, without giving too much thought to existential issues. We explore. We gain independence. We find mates and raise children. We're really freakin' busy.

2. **OMG**: Somewhere in mid-life, we begin (maybe because of a life event like losing a parent) to ask ourselves the big questions. As the questions become more important, the answers still elude us. This creates anxiety, fear, uncertainty and a desperation to figure it all out.

3. **Stay the course**: After a time (I'm guessing five to fifteen years) of searching for answers, they begin to appear to us. Think of a dark room. You find the light switch, but it's on a dimmer. You turn the knob very slowly – and the room very gradually lights up. After a time, the room is bright – and everything in it is easily visible.

Once you've fixed your "purpose compass" you journey forward with confidence – as if your "life sailboat" is headed toward a fixed point on the horizon. This brings a sense of calm and peace. The existential directional struggle has been resolved.

Finally the butterfly has wings

Do you remember learning about metamorphosis in grade school? There's an insect egg. It hatches and out comes a larva. The larva eventually turns into a pupa. Finally, the pupa opens, the butterfly emerges and unfolds its wet, sticky wings.

To me, the meaning and purpose journey is the emergence of the butterfly that is you and me. We finally reach a point in our life's development where we have reached our final stage. Our deep identity is very clear. We will remain in this state for the days that we have left on this earth.

This is important stuff to someone who's gone through it. It's important to your donors of a certain age/stage. I think that we as fundraisers need to be highly tuned to the metamorphosis of meaning to form deep donor connections.

Ken's purpose

A while back, I was approached by my friends and colleagues Tony Myers and Jon Dushinsky to contribute to a book they wanted to create. The big hairy of the idea of the book was that seven different fundraisers from different countries would each choose an important word related to philanthropy – and then write a chapter about that word. The working title at the time was *Philanthropy in Seven Words*.

I loved the idea. I was flattered to be invited to contribute something. I was eager to get going.

After a time of mulling it around, my word became clear. I wanted to write about the word "meaning". I also wanted to tell someone's story to illustrate the importance of meaning to philanthropy – so I asked an old friend Ken Shipley if I could write about him.

He agreed – after asking the modest question "why would you want to write about ME?"

I wrote a long story about Ken's life in philanthropy. About he and Carol taking their four teenage children to Botswana on a CUSO assignment. About his many voluntary roles (Ken and I sit together on the Board of Directors of the Peacefund Canada Foundation). About why he's given so much of his money to so many causes and organizations over the decades.

I sat in Ken's living room one morning and interviewed him and Carol. We sat and talked for about two hours. At the very end I asked him, "Imagine your life if I could reach back in time and take all of your giving and volunteering out of it. What would you have lost?"

He immediately answered "What would I have left?" – to which I responded. "Well, you'd still have your friends, your career, your hobbies, your children and grandchildren."

"But who would my children and grandchildren be?" he asked.

I was gobsmacked. He had given me the perfect response. Ken's course is clear – and he's staying it. He knows who he is. He knows why he's here. He knows his purpose. He knows what gives his life its meaning.

That's why I have such deep respect for this man.

Which D's are we talking about?

In my mind, the meaning metamorphosis involves all three dimensions. Your soul becomes unsettled. You start feeling strong, unsettling emotions. Your conscious mind asks concrete questions – like "why am I here?"

In time, your soul transitions into its purpose. Your itchy emotions are replaced by feelings that are much more peaceful and contented. Your mind comes to understand the outcome – as Ken Shipley's mind had in the little story I just told you.

Your head, your heart and your soul are aligned. You're ready to go back onto life's stage and play your role in the play's final act.

Down to the bone donor-centricity

The point of all this rambling is simply this: Many, if not most, of the donors you relate to are well along this journey of personal meaning. They have wrestled with their existential angst. They have answered many of their questions. They have come clearly to the place of their purpose and meaning in their lives. They know their life elevator speeches.

This returns us to what is becoming a recurring theme in this book. One of the great challenges in philanthropy is that fund-raisers are often a generation (or more) younger than their donors and prospects.

The vast majority of fundraisers I know are still in the "no problem" and "OMG" stages of their lives – while the majority of their donors are in the "stay the course" stage.

If we are to be fully effective at connecting with these donors (as people!),

"We need to understand the 'stay the course' stage of life – and be able to speak its language."

So let's get practical

Here are some of the lessons I've learned about incorporating purpose and meaning into the work I do – and some tips as to how you can bring these elements into the work you do.

Let's look at some examples of how those of us who are still in the 'no problemo' or 'OMG' life stages can engage and communicate with donors who are in the 'stay the course' phase of life.

1. You're updating your charity's web content on legacy giving. You've decided that you want to include a couple of testimonials from donors who have made bequests to your organization. The donor interview and the testimonial that results might yield some web copy (or video) that sounds like this:

"My life has always centred on caring for children. I was the eldest of seven growing up, and it seems I was always the second mother in our household. I raised three children of my own – and taught elementary school for 41 years. I've been so lucky. My life has been full of laughter, love and joy because of all the wonderful children I've gotten to know so well. I've also sponsored children through World Vision for the past 27 years – and that has been a source of deep satisfaction to me.

Caring for children has brought such meaning to my life. It has made me feel that I'm a worthwhile, caring person. My bequest to World Vision will continue my life's purpose even after I'm gone. Even though I won't be here in the flesh, my love for children will live on. To me, this is a noble way in which to end my journey through this life."

2. Your board chair is going to speak briefly to your annual general meeting. Several key donors and volunteers are going to be attending. The board chair asks you to write his speech because he says he's a hopeless public speaker. So, you write something up for him.

"All of us here at the Humane Society have been through a challenging couple of years. The economic recovery is still fragile, and donations aren't growing the way we'd wished for. We've been inundated by an overflow of abandoned and rescued animals – far above what we'd budgeted for.

Having said that, I wouldn't trade my last two years as the Chair of your Board of Directors for anything. I work with a wonderful team of volunteers and staff. I've come to know many of you personally – and that's been a true gift to me.

But, like you, I'm here because of the animals. I grew up with dogs and cats as a child. Sometimes, they were my best friends. The animals in my life have given me so much love, approval and friendship. They have all been such gifts to me. Doing something constructive to better the lot of abandoned, abused and neglected animals is one way I can give back to them. This work means a lot to me. It helps give my life great meaning – and true fulfillment.

Thank you for allowing me to lead this wonderful organization. I consider it a true privilege."

3. You're writing a thank you note for donors who have made a first-time gift in response to an email appeal. The original solicitation was from your NGO's program director in Zimbabwe – and the thank you letter will go out over her name as well.

In the thank you email, you include this text:

"I went to Zimbabwe to give of myself. To do something for others – and to do my own small part to make this world a better place. I was ready for the living conditions and the heat and the lack of material comfort.

But, I had no idea how deeply I would come to love the people. How grateful I would come to feel for the honour of knowing them. How deeply and profoundly this experience would change ME. My life has changed because of Zimbabwe. I have found my calling and my purpose. I want to give – and receive – like this for the rest of my life.

You – and many like you – have made this possible with your generous gift. No doubt you gave to help desperately poor people. And help them you have. But, without intending to do so, you have given me a great gift as well – and for that I thank you."

4. You're planning to visit a bequest prospect in her home. She sent in a direct mail gift and asked for more information about planned giving. You sent the package, and during your follow-up phone call, you asked if she might like to meet in person. She invited you over for tea – and some talk.

    Rather than anticipating what you're going to tell her, you decide to prepare some questions that you want to ask her.

- *What first got you interested in the United Way? Do you remember the first time you made a donation?*

- *Now that you've been a donor for such a long time, what does it mean to you to be a United Way donor?*

- *Would it be fair to say that your community giving and volunteer work is an important part of your life?*

- *It sounds to me that your giving and volunteering give great meaning to your life. Would that be a fair thing to say?*

(The important thing to do when asking questions like these is to see them as prompts. You're not so much asking a question in search of an answer. What you're really doing is inviting the donor to tell you a story. Once she starts talking, stay quiet for as long as you can!)

5. You're the person assigned to write cover letters that will go with the case statement document as part of your capital campaign. The case statement is being sent to campaign prospects who have shown initial interest to a member of your campaign cabinet. Your objective is to bring the prospect one step closer to the decision to make the gift. The case statement does a great job of outlining the project and its benefits to the University. You want the cover letter to make the package a little more human.

This new residence building will house 362 undergraduate students for the next century. For many of them, this will be their first home away from home. It will be a place where young people will make lifelong friends, fall in love and find their passions for teaching, politics, journalism and engineering. This place will see much laughter and many tears. It will hear heated debate and hushed whispers. Memories will be made here that will live in these students for the rest of their lives.

Your gift to the Mackenzie Residence Building campaign will make you a part of the future of this campus for decades to come. Not only will you help us pay homage to Madeline Mackenzie – who was so dedicated to this University for 52 years. You will have the satisfaction of knowing that bright minds wake up there every morning and find their sleep there every night. They will have this home in which to grow because you believed in their future. What a meaningful and noble act that would be.

The 100th birthday wish

Imagine that you live to be one hundred. Your friends and family throw a big party. After you blow out your hundred candles (if you can!) people start to make short speeches about you. Looking ahead to that day, from where you are now, what would you want them to say about you?

I've given some thought to this question. I'll share my answers with you now – and I'd love it if you would get in touch and tell me yours.

First off, here's what I hope they WON'T say about me:

- He is one of the smartest guys I've ever known.
- He had an outstanding career and wrote six books.
- He was respected in the philanthropy world for his talent and expertise.
- He always dressed really well and lived in a beautiful home.
- Fraser knows how to manage a dollar.

Now, here's what I WOULD like them to say:

- He has always been free with his knowledge, his interest and his humour.
- I've learned so much from him.
- He has that rare understanding that we must be kindest to those who we think deserve it least.
- He raised amazing kids – and has enjoyed being a grandfather more than anyone I know.
- He still doesn't think he's too old to learn a thing or two.
- Fraser knows that there's nothing in life as precious as love.

Will people actually say those things about me when I'm an old man? Probably not all of them. But I've still got some time to work on it.

The 100th birthday exercise is one I highly commend to you. Because, once you know the answer to the "what do you want them to say about you" question, you've pretty much nailed your own life's meaning and purpose.

Finally, a brief but profound thought from Mohandas Ghandi: *"Where there is love, there is life."* I couldn't agree more.

Chapter 14
That Vision Thing

Given my job, I have the opportunity to walk into the foyers of many Canadian charity offices. Most of these lobbies have plaques or laminated posters on their walls that proclaim the organization's vision statement, mission statement and values to all those who come to visit.

Great idea! But not so great in the execution – at least to me.

Why? Because the vast majority of these statements really suck. In fact, rather than motivating me, many of them are a real turn-off. That's because they don't do their job.

What IS the job in question?

- Your vision statement INSPIRES your constituents.

- Your mission statement MOTIVATES your constituents, and

- Your values/beliefs are the MIRROR in which they see themselves.

Think back to when you were a kid – or better yet, a teenager.

If you were anything like me, you probably heard your mom say a thousand times, *"the fact that the other kids are doing it doesn't make it right for YOU."* And, if you're a parent of a teenager, you probably hear those words pass your lips lots of times too.

Yet, this is precisely what I believe most charities do. The new board chair comes to the charity's office. He sits down with the executive director and says, *"How come we don't have our mission statement on the wall in the lobby? I was at the United Way the other day and they have their mission statement up. I think we need to do that."*

The executive director wants to be onside with her new boss – so of course she says *"That's a great idea Ralph. Why don't we have a board retreat in March? We can do some strategic planning – and work out our vision and mission statements."*

I.   *VALUES? OR BELIEFS?*

The charity I've just told you about holds its board retreat. At one point, the vice-chair pipes up and says, "Don't most charities have their values on the wall too?"

Heads nod knowingly. They agree that they need a values list too. So they spend some time making a big list of "value words" and eventually whittle the big list down to six words.

Those words end up being:

RESPECT	INTEGRITY	TRANSPARENCY
COMMITMENT	DIVERSITY	ACCOUNTABILITY

What do those words mean? Do those words really define the organization's identity? Do they shape vision and mission? Are they any different from the other six charities that have offices down the street? Do those words help donors feel like they really belong with this charity?

My answer to all of these questions is a simple and unequivocal no.

The mirror

Why do I say that your statement of beliefs should act like a mirror? Because, when your potential supporter reads your beliefs, she will (hopefully!) say to herself – "hey, I believe that too."

"Beliefs are the glue of human relationships."

When we are on the same beliefs page as another, we are power-fully connected. And, that connection has great durability – because beliefs (unlike emotions) don't change on the hour. Our beliefs are built to last.

Human beings are tribal animals. We need to belong to a group. We need to experience connection with others. It's in our DNA. Tribes share beliefs. Their shared beliefs are a major source of tribal unity.

- The socialist tribe believes in collectivism. The libertarian tribe believes in individualism.

- The Christian tribe believes in the Holy Trinity. The atheist tribe believes that being human is as far as life goes.

- The kindergarten tribe believes in Santa. Their teacher tribe has a different view.

- The hippie tribe believes in peace and love. The National Rifle Association tribe believes in the right to bear arms.

Our tribalism is very much a two-sided coin. We need to join a tribe that shares our beliefs – whether our tribe rides Harleys, practices yoga, loves anime or eats vegan food. Our tribal membership seems to be made stronger in the presence of another opposing tribe.

- The pro-life movement is stronger because of the pro-choice tribe.

- Kids who pierce and tattoo a lot are bound together by parents and teachers who disapprove.

- Where would Al Qaida be without the U.S. government and military?

What does the man upstairs think?

Several years ago, I read a fascinating book called *New Revelations – Conversations with God* by Neale Donald Walsch.

In this book, an ordinary man is talking to himself. In his conversation, he asks himself a question – and is blown away when God answers his question.

A very long conversation between this man and God ensues...

The one little piece of this book that stands out most vividly to me is when God says something to the effect of *"People act in accordance with their beliefs. If you want to change people's behaviour, you have to change their beliefs."*

I'm totally on the same page as God on this one. We do what we do because of what we believe.

- As I write this, my wife Jennifer and I are watching a fascinating TV series called *Finding Sarah*. It follows Sarah Ferguson, the Duchess of York, as she tries to rebuild her life after making a total mess of it. Here's someone who lived the dream. She married a prince and had two beautiful daughters. If Princess Diana was Diana Ross, 'Fergie', was the Supremes. Then came the nude photos. The tabloids questioning her marital fidelity. Finally, an enterprising reporter caught her in a sting in which she offered to take bribe money in exchange for access to the Royal Family. In the TV series, Sarah is coming to realize that she sabotaged herself because she didn't BELIEVE she deserved the life of a princess. At the age of 51, Sarah is trying incredibly hard to learn to believe in herself. And what a struggle that is.

- In 1996, 25-year-old cyclist Lance Armstrong was diagnosed with stage 3 testicular cancer. The cancer has spread to his brain, his lungs and his abdomen. The oncologists estimated his chance of survival at 40%. Not only did Armstrong survive – he went on to win seven consecutive Tour de France cycling races (1999-2005). The Tour de France may well be the most demanding athletic event known to humankind today. To dominate it for seven years was unimaginable before Armstrong did it.

  Armstrong is someone who clearly believes in himself – and who has big purpose to his life. He has gone on to publish his autobiography (a massive bestseller) and he created Live Strong Foundation – a gazillion dollar cancer charity. This man believes that life means something.

"ANYTHING IS POSSIBLE. YOU CAN BE TOLD THAT YOU HAVE A 90% CHANCE OR A 50% CHANCE OR A 1% CHANCE, BUT YOU HAVE TO BELIEVE AND YOU HAVE TO FIGHT."
                                        - LANCE ARMSTRONG

- My mom was pretty incredible in many ways. She had a genius for people. Her social intelligence was off the charts. She could meet someone for the first time and become close friends within five or ten minutes. My mom had a belief that guided her relationships – especially with new people. She believed that each and every one of us is born with great gifts and great challenges. She believed that the key to a close relationship is for one to celebrate the gifts in the other – and to help the other with his or her challenges.

Isn't that pretty much what we do when we practice our philanthropy? We see the worth in the homeless. We see the potential in the child in Malawi and offer to help her overcome her material challenges. We see the incredible potential in a child with cystic fibrosis – and we give to research to help give him a better chance at a longer life.

I've incorporated as much of this belief into my own life as I'm able. I'm doing my best to pass it on to my children. Their lives will be so much richer if I succeed.

Our beliefs dictate our behaviours. This applies to organizations as well as to individuals. If I know your beliefs, I can predict your behaviours to some degree. This allows me to trust you a little more. Trust is a precursor to loyalty.

I'm offering you the idea that charities should state their beliefs to their constituents and potential constituents. These beliefs should be articulated clearly, powerfully and soulfully. Say this stuff right and you're well on your way to a deep human connection with a potential supporter.

Kiva gets it

Kiva is a smart, innovative charity that leverages the power of the Internet to enable people like you and me to make business loans of as little as $25 to would-be entrepreneurs in the developing world.

When I first visited the Kiva web site in 2009, I was thrilled when I found a simple, direct beliefs statement:

Kiva was born of the following beliefs:

- *People are by nature generous, and will help others if given the opportunity to do so in a transparent, accountable way.*

- *The poor are highly motivated and can be very successful when given an opportunity.*

- *By connecting people we can create relationships beyond financial transactions, and build a global community expressing support and encouragement of one another.*

I'm now a Kiva lender for three reasons. I love the idea of lending money to someone with a face and a name. I think the folks at Kiva simply came up with a brilliant idea at exactly the right time. And – perhaps most importantly – I share their beliefs.

If Kiva delivers on their promise, I'll be with them for a very long time.

You've gotta start somewhere

If your organization doesn't have a compelling statement of its beliefs, why don't you make one? Pick a day next week. Book a meeting with yourself in your calendar (hopefully at your "smart" time of day). Then, spend an hour or two listing three of four fundamental beliefs you think the people in your organization share. Then, just start showing it around and asking for opinions.

You never know. Your words might be on the foyer wall someday. Even if they're not, you're going to have a deeper understanding of your cause, your organization and why you all do the good works you do.

2. <u>*VISION*</u>

Presidential vision fumble

George H. W. Bush was President of the United States from 1984 to 1992. For eight years, he was the most powerful leader in the world. Great leaders have vision, right?

Not so with President Bush the Elder. During an interview on CBS, he was asked why he always focused on short-term tasks and rarely talked about his long-term vision for America.

He responded; *"Oh yeah – the vision thing. I don't really spend a lot of time thinking about that."*

Reaction from the world's citizens (including me) was shock and disbelief. Here we've got the man driving the biggest bus in the world – and he doesn't have a particular destination in mind!

So what IS vision?

For any leader, the organization's vision is its ultimate destination. Ghandi's vision was the peaceful realization of Indian independence from Great Britain. Martin Luther King's vision was equality, respect and love between America's black and white races.

Vladimir Lenin's vision was a singular global communist government and economy – while John Lennon's vision was global peace and love.

For a charity, a vision statement is a descriptive statement of what the world (or your community) looks like when your work is done. When you're ready to close your organization's doors for good because there's nothing left on your agenda.

And why does vision MATTER?

Now we get down to brass tacks. I think many vision statements are lame because their authors didn't understand their value.

A vision statement is NOT something that comes out of a board strategic planning retreat that everyone in the room can agree on. Vision statements often emerge on Sunday afternoon as people are getting tired and looking at their watches – anxious to get home. Sooner or later they say '*Okay, this version's good enough. Let's go with it.*'

 A vision statement IS a description of the future that donors, volunteers and potential supporters can be INSPIRED by.

The word "inspire" literally means "in spirit". It's a soulful word. Not a brain word. So, your inspirational vision statement must resonate with my soul – more than make sense to my brain.

I'm obsessive (as should you be!) about building donor loyalty. Loyal donors are the economic engine of any charity donor database I've ever known. Offering an inspiring vision is a great way to sow the seeds of that precious loyalty.

RNIB gets it

The Royal National Institute for the Blind in the UK has a vision statement I really like (even though they don't call it a vision statement):

> *RNIB wants a world in which blind and partially-sighted people enjoy the same rights, freedom, responsibilities and quality of life as people who are fully-sighted. This vision will always be at the heart of what we do and what drives us forward.*

What I like most about this statement is the second sentence. To me it speaks of commitment and consistency – two things each of us wants in all our relationships. Nice work guys.

Have a rip yourself

So why don't you take a couple of hours sometime this week and sneak away from the office? Find a joint that serves great coffee. Plunk yourself down with your laptop – or a notepad and a pencil for that matter – and write your organization's vision. Write it like it matters. Write it as though everyone will see it and form their opinions of you by what you say. Make it sing. (If you like it, please send it to me. I'd love to have a look and give you my two cents worth!)

3. *MISSION*

The mission to end all missions

On July 20, 1969 I – like the rest of the world – was transfixed to the television. Apollo 11 had landed on the moon. Its Commander, Neil Armstrong, became the first man to walk on the surface of the moon.

To a 14-year-old boy, that was one of the magic moments of my life. I remember looking up at the moon at night for weeks after – thinking to myself "my God, we were just walking there!"

Did that mission excite me? You bet it did. Did it inspire me? Absolutely.

Almost a decade earlier, US President John Kennedy made his mission statement when he said, "I believe that this nation should commit itself to achieving a goal, before this decade is out, of landing a man on the moon and returning him safely to earth."

So what IS mission?

For any leader, the organization's mission is the work it does in pursuing its vision. Ghandi's mission was non-violent resistance. Martin Luther King's mission was to build a constituency – black and white – that would make civil rights inevitable in America.

Bolshevik Lenin's mission was worldwide revolution – while Beatles Lennon's mission was to touch people's souls with music and lyrics.

For a charity, a mission statement is a compelling description of what you do in pursuit of your vision. It's a powerful call to arms (metaphorically speaking) for those who share the vision to come to the aid of the cause. It is, in part, an invitation to donate, to volunteer – to advance the cause through the organization's good works.

And why does mission MATTER?

Here's where the rubber hits the road. I think many mission statements end up sounding lame because their authors didn't understand their value.

A mission statement is NOT a clinically accurate description of your services and programs. A mission statement IS a powerful rallying cry that donors, volunteers and potential supporters can be *motivated* by; something that lights the fires of *enthusiasm* among everyone in your constituency.

 We've discussed how important it is for charities to connect with their donors' heads, hearts and souls. The word "enthusiasm" literally means "in the presence of God." It's a soulful word. Not a brain word. So, your motivational mission statement must reso-nate with my soul – more than add up in my brain.

A gold star for CHF

CHF – Partners in Rural Development – is a Canadian international development NGO. Here's how they describe their mission on their web site:

> *CHF is a nonprofit organization dedicated to enabling poor rural communities in developing countries to attain sustainable livelihoods.*
>
> *That's our mission. However, those words don't express all that we bring to it — the passion for change, the determination to produce visible results, and the commitment to ensure that every single person who has anything to do with a community has the opportunity to make it a better one.*

Frankly, the first sentence is pretty much NGO blah-blah in my opinion. But the second paragraph? The organization comes alive! I feel a little jolt of enthusiasm. I like the people already. I feel like I'd like to be a part of this tribe.

As my friend Tom Belford of *the Agitator* likes to say, "CHF – you deserve a raise!"

4.   REPORT CARDS

Let's close out this chapter by randomly picking two charities – and seeing how they do in the beliefs/vision/mission department.

Royal National Lifeboat Institution

My wife Jennifer has a little yellow RNLI gum boot (or "wellie" as they're known in England) attached to her key chain. The Royal National Lifeboat Institution is one of the best-known charitable brands in Britain. These guys drive around in little boats and rescue people who've had mishaps at sea. I've just logged into the site – and here's what I've found...

Beliefs:

 Although RNLI calls them values, the beliefs aren't hard to find. Among other things, the RNLI believes in

- putting the lives of others first
- putting the needs of the team before the individual
- being totally dependable and available whenever they're needed
- being totally transparent and accountable to donors and the public (RNLI doesn't take government funding).

All in all, I think this is pretty good. Grade B

Vision:

> *"To end preventable loss of life at sea."*

Accurate – but oh so lame.

How about something like...

> *"Anyone, anytime, anywhere in the UK who faces emergency at sea will know that the brave volunteers of the RNLI are on their way. In their moments of greatest fear, these victims will take comfort in knowing that an RNLI boat is close by and will be there soon."*

As for grade, I feel generous in giving them a C minus.

Mission:

Here's how the RNLI site defines their mission:

> *"The RNLI is the charity that saves lives at sea. We provide, on call, a 24-hour lifeboat search and rescue service and a seasonal lifeguard service."*

This doesn't go far enough. Where's the focus on the volunteers coming to the rescue? Think of volunteer firefighters risking their lives to save your home or your children from fire. There's a lot of courage and heroism to articulate here. It's lacking.

My grade for mission is a C+.

A final message to the RNLI folks. You're terrific! People in Britain LOVE you! Go ahead and blow your own horn a little louder (okay, a LOT louder). It's not being boastful.

United Way of New York City

Beliefs:

I had to sort through some stuff to get there, but this outfit has a strong belief platform upon which to build vision, mission, strategy and programs.

In essence, UWNYC believes that:

- each and every one of us has a role to play in building our own city

- when we give to our city, we make our own lives better in turn

- social problems must be tackled at their roots because symptomatic solutions don't last

- the right combination of people, money and ideas can achieve great things

- everyone at UWNYC must be brave enough to be accountable for their programs, their spending – and the results they generate.

Note: the beliefs as I've stated them don't appear on the site verbatim. I've interpreted site content to have it make sense in the context of the exercise.

All in all, I'm right in line with what these people stand for. Sign me up as a bona fide tribe-member.

I just wish they'd say things more clearly and directly!

I'll give this component of the site a B. (The thinking behind it is A-worthy!)

Vision:

Aaaarrrgggh!

The site has a section called mission and vision. And yet, I can't for the life of me find the vision.

They could write some beautiful stuff about how much greater an already-great city could be. But they don't.

Grade – F (Come on guys. Get in the game!)

Mission:

The UWNYC articulates a mission statement that's easy to find. Here goes:

> *"United Way of New York City connects people, resources and ideas to create a thriving community characterized by income stability, educational success, and healthy people."*

I'm kind of torn on this one. I get what they're saying – but I don't think they're saying it as well as they could. Words like "resources", "thriving", "income stability" and "educational success" all sound like jargon to me. (Being a MSW type myself, I'm guessing that this was written by someone with a social work degree. The problem with this is that 99% of the donors they're trying to appeal to didn't study social work at university.)

If the role of mission is to motivate me to get involved, this statement doesn't do it at all. This statement needs some humanity, heart and soul – big-time.

Grade – C minus – Right Idea. Wrong expression of that idea. Time for a do-over.

Lights under bushel baskets

The RNLI and the United Way of New York City are great organizations. They're clear on who they are and what they do. They know when, where and how they make the world a better place. They matter.

So does your organization. Otherwise, you wouldn't be there.

The challenge the sector faces is that we don't say this stuff well (if we bother to say it at all).

> **"Being clear on who you are and what you stand for matters to your donors."**

The majority of potential donors – and at least 90% of potential major donors go to your site to help them make their gift decisions.

So please. Take a little time. Get it right. Say it loud and proud.

Your organization will make more money if you do.

Chapter 15

Beauty's Place in Philanthropy

Of all the ways in which we can meaningfully connect with our donors, beauty is surely the hidden gem. Whether you work with the world's poor, the sick, the environment or the disenfranchised, there is great beauty to be found in what you do. That beauty, if properly articulated, can resonate with your donors at a very deep and soulful level.

Even though beauty holds the potential of great connective power, we rarely (if ever) talk about it in the context of our causes or our organizations. This is a huge opportunity – and we're missing it.

This chapter will open the door so that you can encounter the beauty inherent in your good works – and use it to connect deeply, build loyalty and raise more money.

Beauty as experience

Our biggest roadblock with beauty is that we fundamentally misunderstand it. We think beauty resides in something external to us. We look at a Turner painting and think it's beautiful. We feel the same about a sunset over the Pacific, Trevor Pinnock conducting a Bach concerto or the sound of a baby's laugh.

The mindbend I'm about to ask you to do is this: Realize that beauty <u>is an experience that happens inside you</u>. In the deepest part of you. In your soul.

Our encounters with beauty make for the truly special moments in our lives. The moments we live for. The brief experiences that make us feel most awake, aligned and alive.

Let me share three stories with you to illustrate a few of *my* experiences in beautiful moments.

Seeing their eyes

In the fall of 2005, I found myself with time on my hands.

My marriage had ended the previous year. My daughter had just flown the nest to start university in Vancouver. I was learning to live alone again for the first time in almost 25 years.

Along with joining a gym, spending more time with my dad and siblings, buying and reading lots of books and playing my guitars I decided to do some volunteer work. I'd been serving on charitable boards (usually three at any one time) for about a dozen years, but I felt a certain urge to give my time where I would get my fingernails dirty.

For no rational reason I'm aware of, I decided that I wanted to do that volunteer work at The Ottawa Mission – a charitable organization that (among other good works) provides meals and beds to Ottawa's homeless.

So I called and set up an appointment to meet with the volunteer coordinator. I went there at the appointed time, filled out the paperwork – and went in to Diane's office to meet her. We talked a lot about the Mission and its work. She kept asking why I didn't want to volunteer on the fundraising committee – and I kept saying that Ghandi considered spinning cloth as important to him as leading a national independence movement.

We decided that I'd start out in the kitchen – on Fridays from 3 to 6 p.m. I had the suppertime shift – prepping and serving meals.

She took me on a tour of the facility – and of course, she was saying hi to people everywhere we went. She seemed happy to see the "clients". They were definitely happy to see her. Diane just had one of those personalities.

After the tour we went back to her office and sat at her desk. We figured out my start date and were just wrapping up.

Then, the magic moment happened. She looked up at me, gestured out her window and said, *"You know Fraser, out there when you see the homeless, you see the tops of their heads and the palms of their hands. In here you see their eyes."*

I'll never forget that moment for as long as I live.

So I started my volunteer gig. I showed up on Fridays. Signed in. Put on my apron. Washed my hands. Said hi to the other volunteers. Went to see Chef Chris to see what he needed done. He'd give me my job (peeling carrots, breaking 40 dozen eggs, spooning a giant pail of Jello into little bowls. I'd do my prep work for an hour and a half.

Then, at 4:30 we'd set up for service. Three of us would line up behind the counter. Our dinner guests would begin filing in and hand us their plates. One of us would scoop potatoes and vegetables. The next would serve the chicken. The third would ask if they'd like gravy – and ladle it on to the plate where they'd asked for it.

For the next hour, I would serve – and look into a new face every 20 or 30 seconds.

And what faces I saw. I saw pain, sadness and confusion. I saw happiness and eagerness. I saw anxiety. I saw humour and joy.

I saw soulful eyes in grizzled faces. I saw Santa-like mirth in tooth-gapped grins. I heard close camaraderie in the laughter that followed lame jokes. I felt the "coming together" of a family at the Sunday dinner table.

Those moments – hearing those voices and looking into those eyes – were moments of incredible beauty for me. I felt deeply connected to those people. I had been allowed to join their tribe. I felt privileged to be allowed into their safe sanctum.

It sounds cliché, but, during my two-odd years in that kitchen I received much more than I was able to give. I was reminded of a lesson my mom always taught by her example. That there's something special about everyone you meet if you look closely enough. That we're not really better than the other guy – no matter what others tell us. That the most meaningful moments in life happen when we connect with others.

Beautiful morning

This morning, I woke up just before 5 a.m., made an espresso and went out onto the deck of my log house with my two Labrador retrievers. It's been hot this month – but this morning, the temperature made me go back in to get my jean jacket. I sat on my deck and drank coffee with my right hand as my dogs competed for scratches from my left.

I sat for about twenty minutes – and enjoyed the magic of morning:

- It seemed like I no sooner sat down than the conductor tapped his baton and the birds' chorus started up. (My house is surrounded by about 500 trees.)They began to sing just for me.

- The snowshoe hare that hangs out on our three acres came out of the trees and began his clover breakfast on the front lawn.

- The stars were still faintly visible in the grey pre-dawn sky.

- The breeze was barely stirring the wind chimes.

- The biggest tomato in our upside-down planter had begun to turn red. (Mmm – my kitchen will be Tomato City by mid-August.)

- I looked down at my dogs. They'd settled at my feet and were nosing each other in a gentle, grooming kind of way.

- As I pulled out of my driveway about 5:20 a.m., I noticed a sliver of red-orange sun peeking over the eastern horizon.

For twenty heavenly minutes, I'd been saturated in the beauty of a pre-dawn morning, my favourite time of day.

My long-time business partner Jose van Herpt is better at finding these moments than anyone I know. It seems that every time we walk down a street together, she takes a deep breath, sighs, and points to something. Then she'll say *"Look at THAT! Isn't it JUST beautiful?"*

One of my favourite O'Donohue quotes is *"Beauty is the illumination of the soul."* I LOVE that.

Beauty isn't a head thing. It's not even a heart thing. Beauty goes to our very centre. Beauty is an experience of the soul. On that July morning, the beauty wasn't in the birds or the sky or the trees. The beauty was inside me.

Beautiful moment

I remember the exact moment when I realized how deeply I'd
fallen in love with my wife Jennifer. It was just before Christmas
in 2008. We'd met at a yoga class earlier that same year.

She was lying beside me. Gazing at me - just moments from her
sleep.

Her skin was incredibly fair, with faint freckles that would come
back in summer. Her blonde hair was flattened on her pillow. Her
breathing had the slow rhythmic sound of deep slumber, even
though she was still awake.

And her eyes. Oh my God. Her eyelids were slowly half-closing
and half-opening – like a really slow motion cat's blink. I really
saw their colour for the first time. An incredible green that I'd
never seen before – and don't expect to see in anyone else.

Her eyes were safe and trusting. She was in the warm cave with
her mate. She could trust herself to sleep. We were 100,000 years
old. The dangers of the world were out there. We were in here.

That was the first (of many) moments when our souls touched.
And it was one of the most beautiful moments of my life.

Did Jennifer look beautiful in that moment? You bet your life.
But the real beauty was inside me. It was the way my soul drank
up and savoured every last drop of that precious, deep, brief time
with the woman I loved.

Third dimension through and through

Beauty isn't something you think. It isn't something you feel.
It's something you experience in the present moment. And that

experience is your soul lighting up (or illuminating, as O'Donohue articulates it).

I often experience beauty when I'm outside: the "skwitch" of snow beneath my cross country skis; the breeze on my face as I ride my bike; the smell of the river as I kayak in July. I find beauty in music – listening to it or making it. I find incredible beauty in words – those I read and those I hear.

To me, real human beauty is found in eyes and smiles. To meet a face with illuminated eyes and a magnetic smile is a gift. My mom had that face. So does my daughter. So does my wife – when she lets her guard down.

Think of the old saying "Beauty is in the eye of the beholder." It's not in the subject being beheld. It's in the one doing the beholding. That's why there's such diversity in what each of us considers beautiful. Your 'beauty portfolio' is as unique as your fingerprint. No one else on earth experiences beauty exactly the same you do. What you experience as beautiful is an important element of what makes you who you are.

I consider beauty to be a reminder from the Universe; a reminder to let go of the past and the future (where most of us spend the vast majority of our attention) and just be in the moment. Here and now. Where life really is.

Moments spent in the experience of beauty are the most precious moments in life. The moments I find the most beautiful bring out the deepest and the best in me. The real me.

It took me 50 years to learn this. But I know it now. That wait's been worth it.

Out of the closet

"IN EVERY MAN'S HEART, THERE IS A SECRET NERVE THAT
ANSWERS TO THE VIBRATION OF BEAUTY."
– AMERICAN POET AND NOVELIST CHRISTOPHER MORLEY

So why do so few of us talk about the beauty of philanthropy? The
beauty to be found in pursuing our missions and visions? The
beauty in the people involved in our causes?

Are we shy? Do we think it would be presumptuous to go there?
Did someone (a parent or a teacher) drill it out of us in the third
grade?

My soul knows – and so does yours – that we do this work because
of its inherent beauty. Our heads might not be there – but our
souls have always known this. Our donors – especially the older
ones – are no doubt way more tuned in to this idea than we are.

If we want to practice 3D philanthropy, I think we need to bring
beauty front and centre. Dust it off and give it centre stage. Put a
spotlight on it. Make it the star of the show.

Let's do it deliberately, consciously and confidently.

I predict that (like many of this book's ideas) your boss may get
nervous and itchy at the prospect of actually talking about 'the
B-word'. But your donors will love it.

This book is about connecting with donors at a DEEPLY human
level. If you can bring the beauty experience to your donors,
they'll forge a much stronger link with you. From that, comes
loyalty and commitment. And from that commitment, comes
revenue growth.

We must never lose sight of that.

Flashlights on everyone

So now you're aware that there's beauty in your charity's work. You're now tasked with finding that beauty. But the room is dark. I'll hand you a flashlight. Here are some ways to start your search.

- Look for beauty in faces. The faces of the people you help. The animals you care for. The volunteers and donors who make the helping possible. Show those faces. Use photos and video. Last night I visited two CARE websites – and went to the "who we are, what we do" stuff. CARE USA has a photo of a middle aged woman who's largely expressionless. CARE Australia has a photo of a little girl (maybe 5 years old) carrying a baby in a blanket tied snugly-style on her chest. Her expression is pure pride and joy. One photo sucks. One photo sings. One is beautiful (to me at least). One is not.

- Put beauty in your vision statement. Read the vision statement your organization uses now. Ask yourself "is it beautiful?" If it's not, re-write it! Worry about the board approving it later. For now, just write it.

- Capture the moments where beauty is illuminated most brightly. The homeless woman turning the key and walking into her new apartment for the first time. The patient opening his eyes – and realizing he's still alive - after life-threatening surgery. The bursary student accepting his degree from the University Chancellor. The sun rising over the treetops in a forest that's just been turned into a park because of your campaign.

  Show those moments every way you can.

- Do a beauty check-up. (I'm a big check-up guy as you may already know.) Have a look at your website. Grab last year's annual report. Your CEO's speech to last year's AGM. Your last direct mail package.

The thank you letter you're sending to first time donors. Is the beauty there? Is it explicit? If not, start the makeover!

- In your story inventory, make sure there's something beautiful in every story you tell. You can tell about ugly too. Just make sure there's some beauty there too.

(Psst: Here's a tip. Simply start slipping the words "beauty" and "beautiful" into your work vocabulary when you talk to donors. Use them when you write to them, and for them. Just using those two words is a great first step.)

The key lesson in all of this is simple:

The moments in which we experience beauty in our souls are the moments in which we are most alive. Giving your donors moments like these is a gift beyond measure. Give them these gifts and they will richly reward you in turn. Everyone wins – bigtime.

A final thought

In my experience with those closest to me (including myself), the hardest place to find beauty is in the mirror. For reasons I don't even begin to understand, many (if not most) of us simply can't see our own beauty.

Yet, in a larger sense, isn't that what we try to do for others in our work? With the homeless? With the world's poor? With the sick and injured?

We all deserve to be more kind and loving to ourselves. Charity begins at home. And your home is your soul.

In his inaugural address as South African President in 1994, Nelson Mandela said these words. They were written by American author and peace activist Marianne Williamson. I'll close this chapter with them - for you to ponder.

"Our deepest fear is not that we are inadequate.

Our deepest fear is that we are powerful beyond measure. It is our light, not our darkness, that most frightens us.

We ask ourselves, who am I to be brilliant, gorgeous, talented and fabulous? Actually, who are you not to be?

You are a child of God. Your playing small doesn't serve the world. We were born to make manifest the glory of God that is within us. It's not just in some of us; it's in everyone.

And as we let our own light shine, we unconsciously give other people permission to do the same. As we are liberated from our own fear, our presence automatically liberates others."

Ah.

Beautiful. For me, anyway.

Chapter 16
CAUSE and effect

If you want to read this chapter in 64-word short form and skip to the next chapter, here you go:

> *You and your colleagues get saturated with the business of your organization. Your donors care more about the cause than they do about you. Your organization reaches donors' heads. The cause reaches their hearts and souls. Heart trumps head. Soul trumps heart. Organization loses. Cause wins. If you want to raise a LOT more money, keep your focus on the cause. Never forget 60:40.*

(Psst...It's not about YOU!)

In my experience it's almost impossible not to get swallowed by the whale. By that I mean to get so wrapped up in your own organization's comings and goings that you think the world begins and ends within your office's walls.

It's natural. Everybody does it – at least sometimes. It's not your fault.

As a full-time fundraiser with a charity, you're busier than you ever imagined you would be. Tasks, pressures and deadlines swirl around you each and every day. You work incredibly hard at the details of everything on your desk. It's absorbing and time-consuming isn't it?

But there's a potential problem in this – one that I see all the time. You're so wrapped up in your organization and its details that you come to assume over time that your donors are as interested in the nitty gritty as you are.

Guess what?

They're not.

In fact, they may or may not be all that interested in your organization at all.

Let me put it another way. Your donors aren't all that concerned with HOW your charity does its good works. They're more concerned about WHY you do it and WHAT happens when you do it.

Stop and think about your car for a minute. Do you really understand HOW the internal combustion engine works? Do you know in detail HOW anti-lock brakes are made differently than old fashioned brakes? Do you know HOW high octane gasoline is different than regular?

Of course you don't. 99% of us want to buy a car, turn on the ignition, fill it with gas – and go. That's all you care about. (And, that's all I care about too!) You simply want your car to take you where you want to go. The rest is unnecessary detail.

The inside/outside dance

There are two ways that people in advertising, marketing, campaigning and fundraising think about themselves and their constituencies/audiences.

I first learned about inside-out and outside-in from two authors named Al Ries and Jack Trout back in the 1980s. This simple lesson has served me incredibly well over the past 25 years. I want to share it with you now.

Inside-out thinking goes something like this.

> *Our charity has this great program starting up next fall. We need
> to tell our donors about it so that they'll give lots of money to
> support it. The program's strategy and plan is so well thought out
> that our donors are going to love it.*

Outside-in thinking goes something like this.

> *We know that our donors care about our cause. Now that we've
> got this new program, how can we campaign for funds in a way
> that's going to resonate with our donors most strongly?*

There are a few fundamental differences between inside-out and
outside-in.

1.   Inside-out starts with you, while outside-in starts with the donor.

2.   Inside-out starts with assumptions, while outside-in starts with
     questions.

3.   Inside-out is presumptuous and egotistical, while outside-in is
     humble.

4.   Inside-out rarely works as well as outside-in.

In both my political and philanthropic careers, I've had countless
struggles with colleagues on this issue. They want to talk about
'us' – while I encourage a focus on 'them'. I'd say my track record is
a little better than 50-50. This is one hard nut to crack.

It's common sense on Madison Avenue

Advertising students have been taught for years to focus on
benefits rather than features. Car buyers don't want to know how
anti-lock brakes work. They want to know that their car will stop
fast. The mechanics of the brakes are its features. Stopping fast
(and not smacking into that school bus) is the benefit. Donors,

customers, voters all care way more about the benefits to THEM than they care about the smart features that YOU came up with.

Smart marketers sell benefits. The high school pusher sells the high – not the drug. Disney sells fantasy and childhood escape– not movies and theme parks. Harley Davidson sells a throaty roar and masculine ego stroking – not motorcycles.

If you HONESTLY look at your work from the outside-in, it's not hard to come to the conclusion that:

- People give to the poor in their community more than the United Way.

- People give to disaster victims more than the Red Cross.

- They give to abused and abandoned animals more than they give to your local Humane Society or SPCA.

- They give to protect the planet's health more than they give to Greenpeace.

- In all of these cases, the organization is simply the HOW that connects the donor and her money with the cause and the beneficiary.

This is as straightforward as it gets. I guess it's up to you to decide whether you buy what I'm selling. For your organization's sake, I hope you buy in big-time.

My favourite maxim

In my years as a fundraiser, I've picked up lots of smart slogans, witticisms and short pearls of wisdom. The most valuable of them all is a simple five-word sentence.

"The institution has no needs."

If you get one lasting idea or lesson out of this chapter, let it be those five words. It's not about you. It's about your donors. Write these five words down. Pin them up on your office. Put them on your screen saver for six months. Tattoo them onto your forehead. Do whatever it takes to remember them always.

The WHY sniff test

The simplest and most important question to any fundraiser is "why should they give?"

The first answer to that question is that they care about the cause. No one's going to give to the American Cancer Society if they don't particularly care about fighting cancer.

If you don't believe me, ask your donors! (This is what my consulting partners and I have been doing for years now. When we're not sure – or when we can't convince our clients – we hold focus groups and let the donors be the judge and jury.)

So here's the sniff test you can use.

Just starting asking your donors, *"Why did you make your first donation to us?"* I'll bet the farm that their answer will be about the cause – and not about how terrific your organization is. When you ask why they continue to give, you'll probably get an answer that combines the cause and your organization. (Something like *"I really care about people going hungry here in Cleveland – and I know the Food Bank does a great job of feeding the hungry."*

I have yet to meet a donor who answers a WHY question without talking about the cause. And, I've listened to a LOT of donors.

Now, before lots of you start sending me angry emails, let me make one point abundantly clear. I'm not saying that your organization doesn't matter. I'm not saying you shouldn't talk about your programs, your services, your track record or your results. Of course you should do those things. But you must not impinge on the cause's rightful turf.

How this looks in 3D

So let's bring this chapter back to our idea of the three dimensions. Let's follow someone who weaves in and out among head, heart and soul as she makes her giving decision.

> Barb is a dog lover. She has two terriers named Hamish and Winnie who she loves like children. Barb is a crazy-busy professional. Her dogs are her healthy interruption from the demands and stresses of the day.

> One day Barb gets an email from her colleague (and fellow dog lover) Joyce. The email has a link to a recent TV news report about a puppy mill bust. There's footage of these little puppies being loaded onto a Humane Society van.

> The story ends with the Executive Director of the Humane Society saying that their facility is packed to the rafters with abused and abandoned dogs – and that these puppies will have to be put down.

> Barb starts to cry – and reaches for her cheque book.

Let's go back through this story in 3D. Barb has an emotional and spiritual relationship with her own dogs. She looks at the news story. She sees how poorly these puppies were treated at the puppy mill. She feels sad (which is heart) – and also feel a deep empathy (soul) for those poor puppies. Then she gets angry (heart) at the people who run the puppy mill. Next, there's sadness (heart) at the news that the puppies will be put down. Impulsively (heart), she reaches for her chequebook and decides to write a $100 cheque (head) to the Humane Society. Once she mails the cheque, she feels a sense of purpose (soul) and relief (heart) that she's done the right thing.

Let's move this little vignette a few years into the future. Barb has continued to give to the Humane Society. She volunteers to walk dogs two days a week. She's come to know some of the staff and volunteers at the Humane Society. She respects and likes them all. Barb reads the newsletters and annual reports – and has formed the opinion that the organization is well-led and well-managed. She trusts them with her money.

Has she reached the point where she cares more about the institution (the Humane Society) than the cause (animal welfare)?

Nope.

And, she's never going to.

Some personal examples

- From 1992 till 2009, I served on the Board of Directors of the Douglas-Coldwell Foundation. It's a Canadian social democracy think-tank that funds projects that inject new ideas into progressive politics. I've served with some prominent and amazing Board colleagues. The organization was the brain-child of Tommy Douglas – the man who introduced socialized medicine to North America (and was later voted the Greatest Canadian of All-Time because of it.) Tommy is one of my biggest heroes.

Did I serve on that board for 17 years because I was committed to the organization? Did I serve because Tommy founded it? Did I serve because of the love and respect I had for so many of my Board colleagues?

Nope. I served because I'm a social democrat and I felt I could do something small to advance a progressive political agenda in Canada.

- I spent six years on the Board of the Learning Disabilities Association of Canada – including terms as Treasurer, President and Past-President. I continue to make a meaningful monthly gift. I'm a loyal and committed supporter and donor – and I expect to continue to be for years to come.

Why do I give? Is it because of the LDA's great programs and services? Is it because I think they have a superb CEO (which I definitely do)? Is it because I feel invested because of the leadership role I played?

Again, the answer's no. I give because I still have a movie-like scene in my head of a bright 8-year-old girl sitting at the dining room table. She's crying over her homework again tonight. She's as frustrated as can be. She feels stupid. She just feels worthless. My heart is breaking. I'm her dad. I'm supposed to fix it. I can't.

That little girl is the cause. I give for every Canadian kid like her who learns differently. I give so that they can learn – and reach their intellectual and human potential. When these stories have happy endings – as this little girl's has – it's a beautiful thing.

The 60:40 Rule

This rule is simple.

You should spend more time (60%) talking about your cause than you do about your organization (40%). Do this because your donors are – and always will be – more cause-committed than organization-committed.

The cause will always be the place where the donor's heart and soul come alive. Your organization will have to prove credible to the donor's head. No one would argue that. But don't get all fixated on what you're doing. Stay focused on who you're helping and why you care.

Is it time for a cause makeover?

Here's your assignment. Go to your web site, annual report, thank you letter, case for support and your most recent direct mail appeal. Rate each one's 'cause:organization' ratio. If you get 20:80 on your web site, 25:75 in your annual report and 15:85 on your last mail appeal, you've got some work to do.

There's no time like the present!

Chapter 17

Would you buy a ShamWow from this guy?

"THE BEST PROOF OF LOVE IS TRUST."

- JOYCE BROTHERS

In the last chapter, I lectured you in a way that might have made you feel like you and your organization don't matter that much to your donor.

In this chapter, I want to do the opposite.

Let's start talking about trust - the trust between people in a relationship. The trust between donors and the people at the charities they give to.

The anthropology of trust

What exactly is trust? Where does it come from? And, why does it matter so much to us in our relationships?

Let's go back to the cave 100,000 years ago. Our ancestors in that time lived their days in a well-deserved state of fear. Fear of that pride of big lions that's been hanging around the neighbourhood this year. Fear of poor hunting – and the hunger that will result. Fear of the neighbouring gang of cave guys who keep throwing covetous glances at your berry bushes.

So what does someone in constant fear want more than anything? He or she wants to feel safe. And what does safe mean? It means the absence of fear.

If you strip human behaviour down to its simplest level, it's driven by two fundamental states. Those states are love and fear. If you look deeply enough at your own behaviours, you can probably link most of them down to these two drivers.

For example, one of the reasons I work very hard is to ensure that I'll keep my job. I want to keep my job because somewhere deep down, I'm afraid I might lose my paycheque. Losing my paycheque means I won't have enough money to meet my mortgage payment or buy groceries this Friday. I don't want my kids to have their ribs sticking out while they sleep in a ditch.

How likely are these things to happen? Not very. Is the fear real? I think so.

We still desperately want to have relationships with people we feel safe with. Those people (in my experience at least) are not many in number. We tend to place incredibly high value on those trustworthy people in our lives. The ones who have our backs. The ones we can count on.

Trust in three dimensions

So let's deconstruct trust piece by piece.

I want to live free of fear (heart). I find someone –like my wife – whom I can trust. Her behaviours over time tell me that I can count on her (head). I decide to place my trust in her (head). She doesn't let me down. I continue to feel safe with her (heart). Because I feel so safe with her, I start to open up with her and show her my really deep stuff (soul). Our individual selves merge into one in some ways (soul).

It's not complicated.

Turning to your donors

Your donors want to trust the charities they give to. They're giving from emotional and spiritual impulses to help others and build humanity. Heart and soul stuff.

But their heads need to get into the game too. Are you demonstrating objectively that you're earning the trust they've placed in you?

They've taken a risk with their first gift. Will you do what you said you'd do with their money? Will it generate results? Will you be available if and when they have problems or questions?

This is important stuff to you too. If they really trust you, many will become loyal. And loyal donors are the economic engine of philanthropy in this day and age.

Building donor trust is an excellent use of your time, energy and (to some degree) money.

So what can you do to earn it?

Here is a list of eight simple things your organization can do (if you're not doing them already) to build the trust your donors feel toward you. For what it's worth, this list also works on partners, kids, friends and co-workers.

All of the items on this list essentially fall into two categories: honesty and reliability.

1. **Be predictable** (on certain things): Send thank you letters and tax receipts promptly. Send your newsletters regularly. Answer your phone when it rings!

2. **Stay the course:** Keep repeating your vision, mission and beliefs – and keep tying your various communications and solicitation pieces

back to them. Show that no matter what today's subject, the core of the organization remains consistent.

3. **Always be available**: Tell donors (over and over and over again) that you want to hear from them. Give them every possible way to get in touch with you. When they do get in touch, respond quickly!

4. **Keep your promises**: If there's one thing I've learned as a parent, it's how I must follow through on what I say I'm going to do. Talking the talk is empty if you don't walk the walk.

5. **Make promises**: You can't keep promises you don't make. Why not make some? Be explicit. Promise that a project will start in April. Promise that you'll call back when they call. Promise that you'll always try to get best value for the money they entrust you with. (Most charities I know are terrified of doing this. I believe that today's market demands courage.)

6. **Fess up**: One of the best life lessons I learned from my mom is this one: If you screw up, come clean fast. It only gets worse if you don't. This works in life. It's always worked with the donors, members and volunteers I've worked with over the years too.

7. **Make it right**: Another simple mom-type lesson. Clean up the messes that you make. If you screw up, tell your donors what you're prepared to do to fix it. People are very forgiving when they see honesty and contrition. (When done really well, fixing screw-ups can actually BUILD trust and loyalty.)

8. **Forget about perfection**: No one expects you to be flawless. Do the best you can do. Be honest about what you did and didn't do. What you can and can't do. Donors LOVE transparency.

This little checklist is of the "everything I need to know, I learned in kindergarten" genre. No rocket science here. Just great fundamentals for building trust, loyalty and revenue.

Trust, loyalty and the revenue they create are what 3D Philanthropy is all about.

"THE BEST WAY TO FIND OUT IF YOU CAN TRUST SOMEBODY IS TO TRUST THEM."

– ERNEST HEMINGWAY

Chapter 18

Lingo-babble

Do you remember the *Far Side* cartoons by Gary Larson? I absolutely love them.

One of my favourites is a cartoon in two frames. In the first frame, a man is standing sternly in front of his dog. The man is pointing into the dog's nose. The dog is looking inquisitively up at his master. Here's how it reads:

what we say to dogs

Okay Ginger, I've had it! You stay out of the garbage! Understand Ginger? Stay out of the garbage or else!

The second frame has the identical cartoon. Only the caption is different.

what dogs hear

Blah, blah, blah, blah, blah Ginger! Blah, blah, blah, blah! Blah, blah Ginger? Blah, blah, blah, blah, blah!

Without realizing it, we often talk to our donors just like that man talks to his dog. A whole lot of blah, blah, blah.

We humans are creatures of language.

Being the highly social animals that we are, language is critical to our ability to connect, communicate and survive.

Using the right language is also necessary to cut through today's clutter. That donor you're trying to connect with is being barraged with thousands of messages today – many of them meaningless marketing jingles, slogans and drivel.

Language is an absolutely key ingredient in 3D connecting. Use the right words and you can create an 'aha' in the brain. Touch an emotional nerve. Ignite a light in the soul. Use the wrong words, and you start the lingo-babble.

18 words that drive me nuts

Let me be clear. It's not the words themselves that drive me to distraction. It's when we use them out of laziness because we can't or won't take the time to think about what we really want to communicate vividly.

Here's my list:

CAPACITY	SYSTEMIC	SUSTAINABLE
EMPOWER	COMMUNITY	RESOURCES
ENHANCE	INNOVATION	DIGNITY
INDIGENOUS	SUPERLATIVE	FACILITATE
PARTNERSHIP	OUTCOMES	DIVERSITY
DEVELOPMENT	SUPPORT	FOSTERING

6 phrases I can't stand

SUSTAINABLE DEVELOPMENT	CAPACITY-BUILDING
BUILDING COMMUNITIES	PATIENT OUTCOMES
FACILITATING ACCESS	PLANNED GIVING!

And then there are all the freakin' acronyms!

A couple of weeks ago, my wife and I were sitting on our deck in the evening. Jennifer's a program director at the United Way of Ottawa – so as you can imagine, we talk shop at home quite a bit.

We're really interested in each other's jobs and we bounce ideas back and forth all the time.

Jennifer's business card reads "Director – Turning Lives Around." Her job involves funding agencies that work with the homeless, people with mental illness and addictions and families in crisis.

I can't remember exactly where we were in our conversation, but suddenly I blurted out "*You know what? Your card shouldn't say 'Turning Lives Around'. It should say 'People in Deep Shit!'*"

We both had a great laugh – and then she reminded me yet again that she thought she was marrying an adult but ended up with a ten-year-old middle child. (Guilty as charged.)

The next night, we were talking about something else – and she dropped a new acronym on me. Now, the United Way (like every large organization I've ever known) has more than its share of acronyms. But this one was new. She said something like "*If we're going to move the PIDS agenda forward, we need to get our stakeholders on side.*" I interrupted, "*PIDS? What's that?*" She replied, "*Why, it's **People In Deep Shit!**"*

We both proceeded to laugh our asses off.

My first grade "technique"

I get to know new (to me that is) charities, NGOs and nonprofits all the time. Every week, I sit with someone for the first time. They may have called me for a million reasons – but usually, they're asking for some sort of diagnosis and prescription related to fundraising and communications.

One of the best parts of my job is to get up that initial learning curve – and I find that an interview-style conversation gets me up that curve the fastest. So, I start asking questions (most of which start with WHY) and listening hard to the answers.

At some point in the "interview" I get lost. It's getting too complicated. So, I often say - *"Wait. I'm getting lost. Could you do me a favour? Could you say that again – but pretend that I'm six years old?"*

The person I'm talking to ALWAYS pauses, and then tells me again. Invariably, I get it the second time.

Why do I get it the second time? It's because the person talking to me has taken a moment to think about who she's talking to.

As a general rule, the biggest lingo offenders are;

- people in international development NGOs (must be all those grant applications that demand technical explanations)

- doctors – especially surgeons

- charities with communications departments down the hall from the people who do fundraising

- universities

The solution is simple

If you want to get a bequest out of my dad, you'd better not make him work to hard. Or worse yet, make him feel like he's not smart enough or sophisticated enough to belong in your tribe.

My dad's a very bright guy. He's in his late seventies. And, although he only has a high school education, he's well read and very articulate. Having said that, if you start talking to him about "indigenous capacity building," "enhancing patient care" or making a "planned gift," you're running the risk of losing his interest.

Think of it this way.

Cultivating a 3D connection with a donor is like the dance of romance.

Imagine that you're on your first real date with that someone special. She's agreed to come to dinner with you. You're finished your main course and it's going great. She's looking at your eyes a lot. She's smiling when you talk. She licks her bottom lip occasionally (a sign of attraction in body language). You're already imagining making a life with her; a house, children.

Then you lift your right hip up off the chair and let a big one rip.

The mood is lost.

Using words and phrases like "sustainable communities" and "empowering the vulnerable" is like letting one rip on a date. Your 3D momentum has been broken. And, once it's broken, it's awfully hard to get back.

Practical steps

So here's my advice to de-jargonize your language and keep your donors engaged:

Go through your organization's stuff: website, annual report, direct mail samples, your thank you letter, your last e-appeal, your CEO's last speech to the Rotary Club

Make a list of your own organization's 18 words and 6 phrases that suck out loud

Write them down

Ask for 15 minutes at your next staff meeting

Show your colleagues the words and phrases – and ask everyone to stop using them so that your donors won't be turned off

Then, send me an email and tell me how it went.
I'll help you if you need it.

This stuff is simple. But life has taught me that simple things in life aren't often easy.

Chapter 19

And they all lived happily ever after

"STORYTELLING IS THE MOST POWERFUL WAY TO PUT IDEAS INTO THE WORLD TODAY."

– ROBERT MCAFEE BROWN,
AMERICAN THEOLOGIAN AND SOCIAL JUSTICE ACTIVIST

Everything you've read in this book can fit into your organization's story. Everything I've written for you was done so that you can do just that. Tell kickass stories. Connect deeply with donors. And make more money.

Let's strip this onion right down to its centre.

We are all simply human beings. Donors are no different. They don't think or feel or experience differently because they're in "donation mode." They are simply people who are in the act of considering – or making – a gift.

Now that you've read the book, I'll tell you my dirty little secret.

This book isn't really about fundraising. Not at all.

It's about people - and how people connect with each other. How we all need relationships and human connection to live fulfilled, happy and purposeful lives.

Become a great people-connector and the dollars will come.

Let me use my own life to illustrate if you will.

Here are a few of the important things going on in my life as I'm finishing this book.

- Next week Jennifer and I are going away together. Just the two of us. I've rented a cottage near the beach in Ogunquit, Maine to celebrate the trauma of her 40th birthday. Jennifer is my soul mate. My comrade in arms. My advisor. My shoulder to cry on. My fellow prankster (big-time). My lover. My fellow traveller.

  The pace that we live at is crazy. We have two boys, two Labs, two cats, and demanding careers. Our parents and all our siblings live within 45 minutes of us. We have many passions, including biking, yoga, cross-country skiing, reading, music, reiki. There's never a spare moment in our lives – or so it seems. We're on the go from 6 a.m. until we turn on the TV (usually to watch something on the Oprah Winfrey Network) to decompress for an hour before bed.

  Now, truth be told, we're both pretty high energy personalities. No one would say that we move like molasses or that we put off till tomorrow what we can do today.

  But next week? We'll take a couple of hours to drink coffee and just talk on the porch in the early morning. We'll go exploring on our bikes till noon. I'll make lunch and we'll have a long nap. Then we'll spend the rest of the day at the beach – watching the Atlantic roll in and feeling the sun on our faces. We'll make dinner and go to bed early. Heaven.

  Once or twice a year, we both manage to slow down and really be in the present moment most of the day. It's heaven. No one helps me slow myself down like she does. I can't wait.

  It took more than fifty years for Jennifer to walk into that yoga class and put her mat down beside mine. She was absolutely worth the wait.

- So that best friend I told you about? Jack? Is coming to Ottawa in just over a week. Jack and I have been best mates since we were fifteen. Jack lives on Vancouver Island – and we don't get to see each other very often.

Jack and I joke together and laugh like crazy men. We sing together for no reason. We talk about life, philosophy and spiritual stuff until the wee hours of the morning. Jack is a fellow seeker – and we seekers seem to be few and far between.

I'm excited to see him again because I miss him. But more than that, this will be the first time that my boys will meet him. Thomas and Zachary have shared their lives with me for two-and-a-half years now. They've heard all about Jack – but they've never been in the same room with him before. They're going to ask him questions like crazy about when he and I were young. They're going to collect incriminating evidence regarding my misspent youth (there's LOTS of that). They're going to hear story after story about Jack's life – and mine. They're going to love it.

Jennifer already knows Jack. We spent a weekend at Jack's house in Nanaimo last year – and you'd think they'd known each other from birth. I can't begin to tell you how deeply happy and grateful I feel that these two incredibly important people in my life connect with each other so easily and meaningfully.

My connection with Jack is one of the great treasures of my life. I celebrate him. I celebrate us. And now that he's coming into my new home to meet the new members of my family, I'm simply thrilled beyond measure.

- My cousin Brock lives in Calgary. We've been close since we were little – and we had our "discovering manhood" summer working on the Nicola Lake Cattle Ranch in British Columbia the summer we were both seventeen.

  Brock is an easy-going, playful guy who has a knack for being in the moment that I envy. When we're together, we're like kids on summer vacation. He knocks on my door in the morning and out we go – to make the adventures of the day.

Brock's just emailed to let me know that he and Karen are coming to Ottawa for a family wedding at the end of September – and that he can take the best part of a week to come and hang out with me.

So we'll play a lot of golf. Drink a lot of coffee. He'll take over my kitchen and BBQ (he's an amazing cook). He and Jennifer will exchange B.C. and Ontario wines – and discuss them in a language I just don't get. (*"A hint of raspberry, oak and citrus"* – what the HELL does that mean anyway?)

Jennifer and the boys already know Brock – and they adore him. Again, I'm so lucky that all the people I love most are just clicking with each other. It's magic to me.

The point I'm trying to make with these little stories is that most of the stuff we worry about all day long isn't really the stuff that matters when it's all said and done.

The quality of our lives is predicated upon the relationships we have with others. The fun, joy and love we share with each other. It's also predicated on the relationship we have with ourselves – but that's a whole other book!

These are the things that matter most to the people who make gifts to your cause and organization. They value human connections. They know what really matters in life.

Does your charity or NGO really matter to your donor? Could it? What would you have to do differently to make that happen? Stories are a great start. The stories you tell to them – and the stories you ask them to tell to you.

You now have lots of ingredients to put into your story recipe. Emotion. Sensual stuff. Powerful vision and mission. A cause that truly matters. Real people speaking from the heart. Think of chapters 9 through 18 as ingredients sitting on your kitchen counter. Pick the ones that you think will taste good together and give it a go.

My deep hope is that this book has given you a new way to look at the good work you do – and that maybe it's unlocked some doors that you haven't ventured through before.

Go ahead. Take a risk. See what happens.

I'm pretty sure you'll be surprised at what happens next.

I'll close this book by quoting one of my spiritual sages, Forest Gump;

> *"Life is like a box of chocolates.*
> *You never know what you're gonna get."*

References

Books

Burnett, K. (2002) *Relationship Fundraising: a donor based approach to the business of raising money.* John Wiley & Sons Inc.

Cacioppo, J. (2008) *Loneliness: Human Nature and the Need for Social Connection.* W.W. Norton & Co.

Jay, E. & Sargeant, A. (2004) *Building Donor Loyalty: the fundamental guide to increasing lifetime value.* John Wiley & Sons Inc.

Schank, Roger C. (1995) *Tell Me a Story: Narrative and Intelligence (Rethinking Theory).* Northwestern University Press.

Walsch, Neale D. (2002) *The New Revelations: A Conversation with God.* Atria Books.

Online documents

Harder, A. (2011). *The Developmental Stages of Erik Erikson.* Retrieved from http://Support4Change.com.

The Gallup Organization (2011) Retrieved from http://www.gallup.com/poll/147887/americans-continue-believe-god.aspx

The Toronto Star (2008) Harris-Decima Poll. Retrieved from http://www.thestar.com/News/Canada/article/434725

A Final Word

No one writes a book in isolation. There are people who are deserving of my thanks and I'd feel serious guilt if I didn't mention them here and now.

Two authors shaped my early fundraising mental framework. Ken Burnett's *Relationship Fundraising* and Mal Warwick's *Revolution in the Mailbox* not only got me grounded, they showed me how powerful a book on philanthropy can be to guide someone new in the sector.

My business partners Jose van Herpt and Leah Eustace are incredible. They understand that I'm a VERY curious puppy who thrives at the end of a very long leash. They have allowed me the time and the bandwidth to focus on this work when I needed to. I'm grateful to them for carrying the weight of us earning a living while I was tucked in the corner of a coffee bar.

Many friends and colleagues previewed chapters and gave me great criticisms, compliments and suggestions. Jon Lloyd and Eric Hebert-Daly gave particularly special gifts of their time, intelligence and energy.

The folks at Equator Coffee Roasters in Almonte Ontario were most tolerant of that unshaven guy in the shorts and t-shirt who showed up daily at 6 a.m. to sit at his laptop in the front corner by the window. Thank you all for the fuel, the great writing space and the superb tunes.

Finally, and most importantly, I want to thank Jennifer Benedict for reading every single chapter with her critical eye. For taking care of house and kids when I disappeared before dawn day after day and for telling me that this book needed to be written. For reminding me that I'm a worthwhile person – and that what I've got to say is worth listening to. If only we all had a Jennifer, this world would be a much, much better place.

Postscript

IN MEMORY OF

JACK LAYTON

1950-2011

Finally, a dedication to someone who has been one of a handful of people I've known who fully lived his life in 3D.

I first met Jack Layton in 1983. I was doing federal pre-election organizing in downtown Toronto – and Jack was a City Councillor who was deeply involved in our federal campaign.

Jack intuitively had the three dimensions in his bones. He was smart and thoughtful. He was engaging, energetic and enthusiastic. But most of all, he had soul to spare. This man simply had a deep concern for his fellow human beings – and an equally deep conviction that we could do something constructive to advance humanity's cause.

In the 28 years that I knew him, Jack always impressed me with his intellect, his passion for social and environmental justice and his boundless joy in social and political activism.

Jack summed it up in a letter he wrote to all Canadians just before he died. The letter concluded;

> *"My friends, love is better than anger. Hope is better than fear. Optimism is better than despair. So let us be loving, hopeful and optimistic. And we'll change the world."*

I can think of no more apt words to leave you with as you close this book.

Thank you Jack.

AT THE END OF THE DAY, 3D PHILANTHROPY IS ALL ABOUT CREATING GREATER DONOR LOYALTY – AND GREATER REVENUE AS A RESULT OF THAT LOYALTY. <P.81>

A self-confessed "market research freak", Fraser Green believes that donors, prospects and members have so much more to tell us if we simply ask them thoughtfully and appropriately.

Fraser is Principal and Chief Strategist at Good Works, a fundraising consultancy that helps charities build loyal donor constituencies. With a unique combined expertise in market research and philanthropy, Fraser's focus is on deep human communication, donor research and legacy giving.

Fraser is a gifted writer and a sought after public speaker. He presents regularly at fundraising conferences in Canada, the USA and Europe. His articles and contrarian rants (as he calls them) are frequently published in professional journals. Fraser is the co-author of Iceberg Philanthropy (2007), and a contributing author of (me)volution (to be published 2012).

Fraser and his wife Jennifer live with their two boys in a log house outside Ottawa. His daughter Rory has finished her BA in political science at UBC and has already started to change the world as a fundraiser in the nonprofit sector.

www.ingramcontent.com/pod-product-compliance
Lightning Source LLC
Chambersburg PA
CBHW051049050726

47592CB00002B/451